IMAGES
IN
MIRRORS

HEDWIG LEWIS, S.J.

2003
GUJARAT SAHITYA PRAKASH
P. BOX 70
ANAND
GUJARAT, 388 001

Imprimi Potest: Jerry Sequeira, S.J.
      Provincial of Gujarat
      Ahmedabad.
      February 10, 1998

Imprimatur: + Stanislaus Fernandes, S.J.
      Bishop of Ahmedabad
      Ahmedabad
      February 16, 1998.

1ˢᵗ edition 1998
3ʳᵈ edition 2003

ISBN 81 87886 34 X

Price: Rs. 70.00; $ 10.00

Published by: K.T. Mathew, S.J. Gujarat Sahitya Prakash, P.B. 70,
           Anand – 388001, Gujarat, India.
Laser set and printed by: S. Abril, S.J., Anand press, P.B. 95,
           Gamdi-Anand, Gujarat-388001, India.

FOREWORD

There is a poignant story by the British writer Max Beerbohm, called *The Happy Hypocrite*. A lord, who is as wealthy as he is wily, vicious and vain, once attends a ballet and falls in love with a ballerina. After the performance, he rushes backstage, finds her, and on his knees begs her to marry him.

She gazes at him intently for a while, then with sincerity in her voice, says, "Your face, my lord, mirrors, it may be, true love for me, but it is even as a mirror long tarnished by the reflection of this world's vanity."

Not one to give up easily, the lord decides to win her over by deceitful means. From a mask-maker he obtains the mask of a saintly face that fits him perfectly. Then, under a false name, he arranges for her to meet him by a lake one evening. While he waits for her, with his mask on, of course, he sees his reflection in the river. He is so impressed by his 'new' face that he decides to reform his life and manners to match his changed appearance.

The ballerina is attracted to him, falls in love, and eventually marries him. One day she tells him that though she finds his face very appealing, she has been wondering why it has such a frozen look.

The lord decides to call off the bluff. He peels off his mask and stands before her, feeling terribly ashamed, and expecting her to be appalled by the sight and flee. Instead, she embraces him lovingly.

Without his realising it, from the moment he reformed his ways, his face began to change, and it now had the appearance of a saint!

This piece of fiction is not far from fact. In life, too, we know that a person's face mirrors his or her character; a person's actions and reactions are revealed in facial expressions. Except for "happy hypocrites", however, who conceal their real personalities behind cleverly designed masks.

This book presents *Images In Mirrors* -- a large variety of people with and without masks. There are hundreds of anecdotes and stories, each like tiny mirrors reflecting the 'human' aspects of life.

We find as many 'characters' in life as faces — an infinite variety. We generally group them under conventional categories for convenience, but there are nuances in each that defeat description. The 'images' portrayed in this book are thus broadly classified. Hopefully, though, to a greater or lesser degree, they will reflect some aspects of one's own personality and the people and situations one encounters.

In other words, most of them are meant to be projections of our self-images, in varying shades, to enable us to 'see' our reflections and to evoke a personal response. A brief exposure, like a flash of sunlight from a 'mirror', will light up our senses, increase our awareness, and motivate us to action. There are contorted mirrors, too, to amuse — and instruct. Obviously, this will entail a lot of 'reflection' on the 'images' in the mirror.

The stories and anecdotes in this book have been reproduced, adapted, or abridged from multiple sources of varied descriptions — life-experiences, books, magazines, newspapers, brochures, calendars, posters, films....

I started collecting anecdotes, stories and quotes, over twenty-five years ago, because I needed them for the various 'youth-camps' I was involved in conducting earlier, and then for my Retreats, homilies, and seminars.

The idea of compiling and publishing them occurred only recently, at the urging of friends. I regret that I cannot give complete references or make due acknowledgments of the items presented in this book, the majority of which are by anonymous writers. But I am grateful to the hundreds of 'authors' whose contributions are used as sources of inspiration here.

Images In Mirrors provides interesting material for writers and speakers, teachers and preachers. The stories can be used for meditation and prayer-services, as well as for general instruction, entertainment and in conversation.

Preparing *Images In Mirrors*, and its companion volumes *Mirrors Of Life*, and *Mirrors For The Heart*, has been an exciting experience. It was like working on a jigsaw puzzle in reverse. There were these hundreds of little pieces of literature which I had to trim so as to fit them together to form a composite picture. Not all the pieces fit perfectly; some can even be transferred to other places in the picture — to provide a different shade of meaning. When one is dealing with 'human Images' the scope is unlimited!

The original idea, and consequently the title for this book, came from a recent incident. While walking on the road alongside the college building, a student accompanying me picked up a tiny mirror that had obviously fallen off from one of the gowns the girls wear at festivals. In a playful mood, he held the mirror up against the sun and sent a beam into the classroom, then onto the eyes of one of his friends to call his attention.

I dismissed the incident as a boyish prank, then, but it later occurred to me that stories are like little mirrors. They reflect the inspiration, the 'ray of light' thrown on them by their authors. This 'ray' enlightens the mind and is used in turn to brighten one's writings and speech so as to attract the attention of others.

You, dear reader, now have these 'mirrors' in your hand. Create your own images — your 'saintly' personalities, if you please. Let your appearance and your behaviour match!

Hedwig Lewis, S.J.

P.S. *Images in Mirrors* is not a Novel to be read at one sitting. It is primarily a book of 'reflections'. Each of the little mirrors represents a unique person and behaviour and deserves careful scrutiny.

CONTENTS

PERSONALITY
PLUS

His life was gentle, and the elements
So mix'd in him, that nature might stand up
And say to all the world, "This was a man."

Shakespeare

A. PHYSICAL ASPECTS

Attitudes

When asked how she still appears young despite her difficult lifestyle, Mother Teresa replied, "Sometimes a good feeling from inside is worth much more than a beautician."

A doctor in a hospital was completely bald-headed. Every now and then one or other of the nurses would tease him about it. He thought he had had about enough and one day he took the opportunity to retaliate. It so happened that all the nurses of the ward were assembled at the reporting counter when he appeared there. One of them passed a comment on his bald head.

"You know, sisters," he said reprovingly, "God made few perfect heads; the rest He had to cover in hair." Then sticking out his chin, he stalked off down the corridor.

Customer: What do you have for greying hair?

Druggist: Nothing but the highest respect, sir.

✳ ✳ ✳

As a beauty I'm not a great star,
There are others more handsome by far;
　　But my face — I don't mind it
　　Because I'm behind it;
It's the folks out in front that I jar.
　　　　　　　　A. H. Enwer

The heavily jewelled woman was consulting a cosmetic surgeon. "What will the operation of lifting my face cost, doctor?" she asked.

"Seventeen thousand rupees, madam."

"This is robbery," she protested. "Isn't there something less expensive?"

"You might try wearing a veil," he suggested helpfully.

John : Why is it that you fat fellows are always good natured?

Jim : You see, we can't either fight or run.

　　　　*The Lord gives us our
　　　　faces, but we must
　　　　provide the expressions.*

Perspectives

The enthusiastic matchmaker assured the client that he had found him a perfect match — a lovely girl who lived down the street.

"Are you by any chance referring to the chemist's daughter?" enquired the eager bachelor.

"Why, yes, of course. You know her, then?" said the matchmaker.

"Who doesn't. You must be out of your mind," cried the exasperated young man. "Why, isn't she almost blind?"

"True. Does that bother you? It's a blessing, really. Most of the time she won't notice what you do."

"But she also has a stammering problem when she speaks."

"I know. But that too is a blessing. She will be too diffident to open her mouth, so you can have peace."

"But she is deaf."

"Which means you can keep your nerves in control; no screaming or shouting will be necessary."

"But it's impossible. Isn't she at least twenty years older than I am?"

"Come now, my lad," protested the matchmaker, clearly disappointed. "Here's a woman with so many gifts, and you have to pick on one little drawback."

> *There are two kinds of people:*
> *those who think there are*
> *two kinds of people and those*
> *who think it's not that simple.*

Resemblances

A man called on his lawyer and said, "I want to sue that man who lives across the street from me. He called me a hippopotamus."

"We can do that," the lawyer said. "When did he call you that?"

"Six years ago," the man replied.

"Six years ago!" the lawyer exclaimed. "Why have you waited so long to file a suit against him?"

"Well," the man said, "yesterday I took the kids to the zoo and it was the first time I ever saw hippopotamuses."

A certain high-security prison photographed the prisoners from four different angles for the records. When an infamous criminal escaped, the newly appointed clerk was instructed to send photographs of the escapee to Police Headquarters in four different districts. Instead of making copies of the front view, the clerk sent copies of the four shots of the criminal to each of the places respectively.

The next day, the Prison Chief received faxed replies from all four districts with almost similar messages: PICTURE RECEIVED. CRIMINAL SHOT DEAD WHILE RESISTING ARREST.

> *There is very little difference*
> *between people, but the little*
> *difference there is makes all*
> *the difference in the world.*

B. SELF IMAGE

Personal appraisal

Brother Matthew, the first disciple of Francis of Assisi, who accompanied the great saint to various places to preach, was tall and handsome. In contrast, Francis was short and plain-looking. Matthew's stature caught people's attention when the pair walked together in the streets, but it was to the saint that everyone turned for guidance and blessings.

One day, curious to find out about Francis' charism, the disciple asked: "You have a good following, Father Francis; people want to see you, hear you, obey you. Why is it so, even though you are neither tall nor handsome nor of noble birth?"

The saint answered: "The world follows me, Brother Matthew, because God wants it that way. People wish to see me, hear me, obey me because they realise I'm doing God's work. This becomes all the more obvious because I'm not handsome, nor learned, nor noble... they know I could not do this work by myself."

He : We had better organise a mutual admiration society. I admire your eyes. What do you admire about me?

She: Your good taste.

> *It is always easy to spot a*
> *person with a lot of personality*
> *— he always reminds you so*
> *much of yourself.*

Charm

A violin virtuoso on a visit to Africa proclaimed that he truly believed that he could play so well that he could actually charm a savage beast. Despite the warnings and pleas of his friends, he decided he would go to darkest Africa, unarmed, with only his violin.

He stood in a clearing in the dense jungle and began to play. An elephant received his scent and came charging towards him; but, when he came within hearing distance, he sat down to listen to the beautiful music. A panther sprang from a tree with fangs bared, but also succumbed to the music. Soon a lion appeared to join the others. Before long, many wild animals were seated near the virtuoso; he played on, unharmed.

Just then a leopard leaped from a nearby tree, on to the violinist and devoured him. As he stood licking his chops, the other animals approached, and asked, "Why did you do that? The man was playing such lovely music!"

The leopard, cupping his ear, mumbled, "Eh, what did you say?"

The French philosopher Fontanelle was once asked by his hostess, "What is the difference between me and my clock?"

Fontanelle, his poise unshaken, answered gallantly, "Dear madam, the clock reminds us of the hours, while you make us forget them."

A beautiful woman is one
I notice. A charming woman
is one who notices me.

Self-adulation

The disciples of an old rabbi crowded around his bed as he lay dying. In whispers they were extolling his unparalleled virtues:

"No one has seen a wiser person since Solomon," said one of them.

"And what do you say about his faith? Isn't it as deep as that of our Father Abraham?" said another.

"I admire his patience, too," said a third. "It is equal to that of Job."

"I believe he had great intimacy with God," said a fourth. "He was just like Moses."

The custodian of the synagogue, who was present there, noticed that the rabbi seemed restless. After the disciples left, he asked the dying man, "Did you hear them sing your praises?"

"Uh, huh," said the rabbi shaking his head.

"But I noticed you were very restless?" said the custodian. "What was it?"

"My modesty," complained the rabbi. "No one mentioned my modesty!"

"When we are 17," said a wise old man, "we worry about what others think of us. At 40, we don't care what they think of us. At 60, we discover they haven't been thinking of us at all."

✵ ✵ ✵

When you're feeling so important,
And your ego is in bloom,
When you simply take for granted
You're the wisest in the room,
When you feel your very absence .
Would leave a great big hole,
Just follow these instructions,
They will humble your soul.
Take a bucket filled with water
Put your hand in to the wrist,
Pull it out, the hole remaining
Is how much you will be missed.

She: Do you love me with all your heart and soul?

He : Uh, huh.

She: Do you think I'm the most beautiful girl in the world bar none?

He : Yeah.

She: Do you think my lips are like rose-petals, my eyes like limpid pools, my hair like silk?

He : Yup.

She: Oh, you always say the nicest things.

> *A Song that never gets an*
> *encore is when you sing*
> *your own praises.*

Duality

Our padre says I'm a sinner,
And John Bull says I'm a saint,
And they're both of them bound to be liars,
For I'm neither of them, I ain't.

I'm a man, and a man's a mixture,
Right down from his very birth,
For part of him comes from heaven,
And part of him comes from earth.

There's nothing in him that's perfect;
There's nothing that's all complete.
He's nobbut a great beginning
From his head to the soles of his feet.
                                    S. Kennedy

Within my earthly temple there's a crowd
There's one of us that's humble,
one that's proud;
There's one that's broken-hearted for his sins
And one who unrepentant sits and grins;
There's one who loves his neighbour as himself,
And one who cares for naught but fame and self.

From much corroding care I should be free,
If once I could determine which is me.
                                    E. S. Martin

Some people profit by their
experiences; others never
recover from them.

Visualisation

A travelling portrait-painter visited a flourishing suburb hoping to get some business. He stopped by a bungalow and asked if he could do a portrait. The lady of the house told him that only her son was at home — and that because he was out of work. Just as she was about to dismiss him, her son came to the door and told the man he would sit for a portrait.

The artist soon realised that he was facing a frustrated young man who had lost confidence in himself. He was shabbily dressed in dirty clothes; his face was unshaved and his hair dishevelled; it was obvious that he hadn't bathed for a few days.

The painter took a keen interest in his work. Finally, he removed the painting from the easel and presented it to the lad. "That's not me," shouted the young man. The artist gently laid his hand on the man's shoulder and replied, "But that's the man you could be."

There was a boy who asked his father how he was born. The father explained that fathers plant seeds in mothers and then babies grow.

The boy thought for a moment, then asked, "Was my picture on the packet?"

> *If you can imagine it,*
> *you can achieve it.*
> *If you can dream it,*
> *you can become it.*

In *Reframing*, the authors R. Bandler and J. Grinder describe a transformation process that takes place through visualisation. At a therapy workshop they had to deal with a woman who had a compulsive behaviour. She was a 'clean freak' who spent hours keeping everything tidy and shining. Her family tolerated all her idiosyncrasies, except her finickiness in caring for the carpet.

The woman would have everyone enter the house by the back door, and nagged them if they did not. She instructed those who came in from the front to remove their shoes and walk lightly. She did not want people to walk on the carpet because they left footprints — not mud and dust, just dents in the pile of rug. Whenever she noticed footprints in it, she would rush off to get the vacuum-cleaner and smoothen the carpet.

During one session the woman was made to do a visualisation. First, she had to close her eyes, and visualise the carpet as clean and fluffy, with not a single footprint anywhere. Observers noticed that all through this exercise the woman seemed to be in the 'seventh heaven' because her face radiated her best smiles.

Next, she was asked to visualise herself as a totally alienated being, alone, deserted by all the people she cared for and loved. The woman's face now turned grim. One could tell that she was feeling miserable. She appeared sad at the end of the exercise.

The therapist then instructed the woman to close her eyes once again, see footprints all over the carpet, and the people she cared for most in the world, nearby, without tension, cheerful. She began to feel good again.

"I must choose between the carpet and my loved ones," she murmured to herself. There and then she made up her mind. Her behaviour changed radically. She didn't bother about the dents in the carpet any more.

✳   ✳   ✳

Self-made

A young priest once remarked to a man noted for his wit, "I am a self-made man."

The wit answered, "That, Father, relieves the Almighty of a great responsibility."

Benjamin Disraeli, a British prime minister, was used to making harsh verbal attacks on John Bright, a politician and orator. Someone once remarked to Disraeli, "You ought to give Bright credit for what he has accomplished. He's a self-made man."

"I know he is," retorted Disraeli, "and he certainly adores his maker."

Pablo Picasso, never known for his modesty, once told an old friend of his mother's ambition for him:

"When I was a child, my mother said to me, `If you become a soldier, you will be a general. If you become a monk, you will end up as pope.' Instead I became a painter and wound up as Picasso."

> *Some people grow;*
> *others just swell.*

Self-consciousness

It was a cloudless morning, yet the spry-looking, elderly gentleman at a bus-stop was carrying a huge black umbrella. A fellow-traveller told him that rain was not expected.

"It isn't," replied the aged gentleman. "Actually, I need a cane. But if I carry one people say, there goes that poor old man! This way they say, there goes that damn fool with the umbrella."

✳

A society columnist asked Bernard Baruch, the financier and statesman, how he arranged to seat the notables who attended his dinner parties.

"I don't bother about who sits where," Baruch replied. "Those who matter don't mind — and those who mind don't matter."

✳

In Walter Scott's novel *Anne of Gierstein*, the heroine, Lady Hermione, is depicted as wearing on her forehead a large superb opal that mirrored her every mood. When she was happy, the stone glowed; when she was angry, it became red.

✳

The judge looked sternly down at the defendant, "Young man, it is alcohol and alcohol alone that's responsible for your present sorry state."

"I'm glad to hear you say that, Your Honour," the man replied with a sigh of relief. "Everybody says it's my fault."

✳ ✳ ✳

Inner resources

The engine of a truck loaded with goods caught fire in a busy
highway. The driver contacted the fire-station of the nearest town
for help. It took some time before the fire-engines arrived on the
scene, so the whole of the front portion of the truck was engulfed
in flames.

When the firemen broke open the back door of the truck, they
discovered that the inside was loaded with four hundred fire-
extinguishers. The driver, who got himself hired to do the job, had
not bothered to find out what he was carrying.

There is a Polish story about a rabbi in Cracow who for three nights
in a row had a dream wherein an angel told him to go to a nearby
city. The heavenly messenger instructed him: "In front of the palace
there, near a bridge, you will learn where a treasure is hidden."
The rabbi went in haste to the city. He approached the bridge in
front of the palace, and told his dream to the guard standing there.

"Strange," said the soldier. "I, too, had a similar dream on three
successive nights. An angel told me to go to a certain rabbi's house
in Cracow, where a treasure is buried in the front right corner of his
living room."

On hearing this, the rabbi returned home and dug the spot
indicated. And he found the treasure.

> *Once we believe we have*
> *elements of greatness within*
> *us, we begin to enjoy living.*

This story dates back to the time when diamonds were first discovered in South Africa. A farmer there was tempted by a visitor who told him tales of how people had discovered diamond mines in some distant place. Eager to seek his own fortune, the farmer sold off his farm and travelled far and wide. He did not find any diamonds. On the contrary, he lost his money, and his health.

Back in his home-town, the new owner of the land one day discovered an unusual stone in the rivulet that ran by his farm, and placed it on his mantelpiece as a curio. A merchant who noticed it, told him that it was one of the largest diamonds he had seen. The owner discovered several stones like it all over the place. Soon his farm turned out to be one of the richest mines in the world.

Once Paganini, the great violinist, took the bow before a performance, but when he picked up his instrument, he froze — this was not his famous and valuable violin. He excused himself and went backstage only to discover that his violin had been stolen and replaced by a second-hand one.

After a moment's deliberation, Paganini appeared before the audience, explained the situation, then added, "Ladies and gentlemen, I will show you that music is not in the instrument but in the soul." Then he played as he had never played before and brought forth music that enraptured the audience.

The applause at the end of the performance was deafening.

> *There are people who never*
> *sing, but die with all*
> *their music in them.*

His magic was not far to seek
He was so human! Whether strong or weak,
Far from his kind he neither sank nor soared,
But sat an equal guest at every board,
No beggar ever felt him condescend
No prince presume, for still himself he bore
At manhood's simple level, and wherever
He met a stranger, there he left a friend.

J. R. Lowell

The statue of David by Michelangelo in Florence is a marvellous piece of art. The shepherd boy's countenance is alert and determined; he stands erect, his shoulders slightly curved in the act of hurling the fatal stone.

The sculpture has a remarkable history. Over a hundred years earlier, a magnificent block of Carrara marble was brought to Florence by a sculptor. While he began work on it, he accidentally cut off so much on one side of the block that it was rendered useless for the design he had in mind. And so he abandoned it.

When Michelangelo discovered the block a century later, his trained eye immediately gauged its potential. The flaw in the piece of marble turned out to be a blessing; he created a figure that could fit into the misshapen block. As it turned out, the famous artist had fashioned one of the world's greatest masterpieces.

> *Treat people as if they were*
> *what they ought to be and could*
> *be, and they will become what*
> *they ought to be and could be.*

C. CHARACTER TRAITS

Integrity

During Traffic Safety Week, a recently recruited traffic policeman on duty at a busy crossroads apprehended a driver for violating a traffic signal. He pulled out his entry book and politely asked to see the driver's licence.

The driver, who happened to be a high-ranking officer in the Police Department, flashed his credentials. The traffic cop glanced at it, then continued making the entry.

Visibly annoyed, the officer said sternly: "Remember, lad, that one day when your name comes up for a promotion, I may be the one in charge of approving it."

Without the slightest hesitation, the policeman offered the senior officer his ticket, and said with a smile: "When it comes to that, sir, please remember that you have one honest policeman in your employ."

At an army camp in a sensitive zone, a young recruit was on guard duty at the main gate. He was given strict instructions not to allow any vehicle in unless it had a special tag. He once stopped an unidentified car which carried a high-ranking official. The officer promptly told the driver to disregard the sentry and drive on.

The guard stepped forward and in a calm voice said, "I'm sorry, but I'm new at this, sir; whom do I shoot? You, sir, or the driver?"

❋   ❋   ❋

When you get what you want
            in your struggle for self
And the world makes you king for a day,
Just go to the mirror and look at yourself
            And see what that man has to say.

For it isn't your father or mother or wife
            Whose judgment upon you must pass.
The fellow whose verdict counts most
            in your life
            Is the one staring back from the glass.

You may be like Jack Horner and chisel a plum
            And think you're a wonderful guy.
But the man in the glass says
            you're only a bum
If you can't look him straight in the eye.
He's the fellow to please —
            never mind all the rest,
            For he's with you clear to the end.
And you've passed your most dangerous,
            difficult test
            If the man in the glass is your friend.

You may fool the whole world
            down the pathway of years
And get pats on the back as you pass.
But your final reward will be
            heartache and tears
            If you've cheated the man in the glass.

Character cannot be purchased,
bargained for, inherited,
rented, or imported from afar.
It must be home-grown.

A young chartered accountant working in a prestigious firm was lured by another company which was offering him the opportunity to make at least three times more than his present salary. The only hitch, he was warned, was that he would have to use unfair means.

The lad asked his mother for her opinion. After a moment's silence, she replied: "Son, you know when I come to wake you in the morning I shake you hard and you don't stir. And I shake you even harder and you give a little moan. And finally I shake you as hard as I can and you open one sleepy eye. I'd hate to come in morning after morning and find you awake."

He turned the job down and has been sleeping soundly since.

A worried woman once visited Mahatma Gandhi with her little daughter to complain that the girl was addicted to eating sweetmeats. She wanted the saintly man to counsel her to give up the harmful habit. Gandhi hesitated, then said he would help, but she and her daughter would have to come again three weeks later.

When mother and daughter returned, Gandhiji took the girl aside and spoke to her about giving up the habit. The mother was grateful for the advice, but before leaving she asked, "Bapuji, why didn't you speak to my daughter when we last visited you.?"

"There's a simple reason," explained Gandhi. "Three weeks ago I myself was addicted to eating sweetmeats."

> *No one will ever know of*
> *your integrity unless you*
> *give out some samples.*

Versatility

Every age produces multi-faceted geniuses that serve as inspirations for the extent to which human potential can be explored and heights reached. Dr Shivarama Karanth was one such 'colossus' who left his stamp in various fields: literature, culture, science, art, oratory, environment, ecology, dance, drama, folklore and journalism.

A self-made man, Karanth's hallmark was originality, be it in thoughts, actions, or writings. He is said to have achieved in a single lifetime what most can merely aspire to in several life-spans! When he passed away on December 8, 1997, one newspaper headline read: "An untimely death for a young man still growing at ninety-six."

Karanth never identified himself with any one group or stream of thought. He was fiercely independent, and never hesitated to call a spade a spade. He returned the *Padmabhushan*, one of the top civil honours of the country, in protest against curtailment of human rights and freedom during the Emergency government. To him, liberty and freedom of thought and action were more important than personal honours.

Karanth was a living legend. His greatness lay in the fact that he was distinctly different from any other. Even in his nineties, Karanth was as sharp as he was seven decades ago, and at times more aggressive and rational. He is one of the most widely criticised, reviewed, analysed and admired writers — he has about 400 books to his credit. His enormous love for nature, his unquenched thirst to explore its mysteries and his relentless zeal for knowledge made him an icon. His autobiography in Kannada, *Several Faces of a Man's Mind*, reads like an adventure.

❋   ❋   ❋

Individuality

When the CEO of a company died, his son took over. Everyone began to tell him that he was very unlike his father.

"I don't think so," said the young man. "In fact, I'm exactly like my father. He imitated no one. I imitate no one."

> If I am I because I am I,
> And You are You because You are You,
> Then I am and You are.
> But if I am I because You are You,
> And You are You because I am I,
> Then I am not and You are not.
> *Rabbi Mendel*

✳

A man on the street ran up to another, slapped him heartily on the back and cried, "Jack, I hardly recognised you! Why, you have gained twenty kilos since I saw you last. And you have had your nose fixed. And I swear you are about two inches taller."

The other man looked at him angrily. "I beg your pardon," he said in icy tones, "but I do not happen to be Jack."

"Aha!" said the first man, "so you have even changed your name?"

✳ ✳ ✳

Uniqueness

One of the character traits possessed by exceptional people is their ability to live their lives in terms of what the Gospel called "a sign of contradiction" to the world — which brings out their uniqueness. Mother Teresa was one such person.

As one of the weekly magazines reported after her death on September 6, 1997: Her humility was burdened by celebrity. She raised millions for her work but lived simply, befriending the rich and famous to aid the poor and anonymous. She was a woman of power in a Church run by men. Although a missionary of Christ, she insisted that God wanted Hindus to be good Hindus, Muslims good Muslims.

One of the editorials in *The Examiner*, Mumbai, said: It is a world, starved of heroes, who put her on a pedestal so high that she was forced to feel the cold winds of controversy and hostility. In death, she would wish to be completely effaced, letting nothing remain but the good work she did.

Helen Keller could neither see nor hear. Yet she became a great public speaker. One night after a lecture someone asked her this question: "If you could have one wish granted, what would it be?"

The questioner thought Helen might say, I'd wish for the ability to see and hear.

But she said, "I'd wish for world peace."

* * *

Self-reliance

> Out of the night that covers me
>> Black as the pit from pole to pole,
> I thank whatever gods may be
>> For my unconquerable soul.
>
> In the fell clutch of circumstance
>> I have not winced nor cried aloud.
> Under the bludgeonings of chance
>> My head is bloody, but unbowed.
>
> Beyond this place of wrath and tears
>> Looms but the Horror of the shade,
> And yet the menace of the years
>> Finds, and shall find me unafraid.
>
> It matters not how strait the gate,
>> How charged with punishment the scroll,
> I am the master of my fate,
>> I am the captain of my soul.
>>
>> *W. E. Henley*

A poor woman was abandoned by her husband and left with no visible means of support. Some free-legal-aid activists helped her appeal to a court. When the case came up for hearing, the judge asked her, "Madam, have you any means of support whatever?"

"Well, your honour," she answered, "I have three, to tell the truth."
"Three?"
"Yes, sir."
"What are they?" asked the astonished judge.
"My hands, my good health, and my God, your honour," came back the reply.

✳   ✳   ✳

Honesty

A lady had forgotten her handbag in a taxi and had given it up for lost. To her surprise, the driver turned up at her doorstep later that day to return her bag. She pulled out her stuffed wallet from it and was about to offer the driver a reward. But he refused it. He had only one request.

"Please tell me," he said, "how much money you have in your purse." The woman gave him the information and the cabman wrote the amount in a notebook.

Then he explained: "I'm keeping track of what it is costing me to be honest."

"My dear, I certainly hope you don't believe your husband when he says he's going fishing. Why, he's never brought home a single fish!"

"That's exactly why I believe him!"

Back home on leave a paratrooper was asked how many jumps he had made. "Only one," said the paratrooper.

"My service record shows 20 but on 19 occasions I was pushed out."

✳   ✳   ✳

There is an interesting conversation piece in *Alice In Wonderland*:

"Then you should say what you mean," the March Hare went on.

"I do," Alice hastily replied; "at least — at least I mean what I say — that's the same thing, you know."

"Not the same thing a bit!" said the Hatter. "Why, you might as well say `I see what I eat' is the same thing as `I eat what I see'!"

"My boy," said the business man to his son, "there are two things that are essential if you are to succeed in business."

"What are they, Dad?" asked the boy.

"Integrity and sagacity."

What is integrity?"

"Always, no matter what, always keep your word."

"And sagacity?"

"Never give your word!"

*There are no degrees
in honesty.*

Responsibility

Count Saint-Exupery narrates an inspiring incident in his book *Wind, Sand, and Stars*. The Count and his comrade Guillaumet were flying mail over the Andes for the government of Chile. One morning his pal took off in the face of a fierce snow storm. Ice on his wings, the heavy snow and terrific winds kept him from rising over the mountains and forced him to land on a frozen lake.

Guillaumet dug a shelter under the cockpit and surrounded himself with mail bags. There he huddled for two days and two nights. When the storm subsided it took him five days and four nights to find his way back to civilisation, crawling on hands and knees in temperatures twenty degrees below zero.

We are told that he overcame the desire to lie down and rest — which would have proved fatal for him — by telling himself that his wife and sons needed him, and that it was his responsibility to get the mail through. He survived, although his hands and feet were so badly frozen that they had to be amputated.

When Saint-Exupery described his comrade's bitter experience and his superhuman struggle to survive, he summed it all up in one sentence: "To be a man is, precisely, to be responsible."

*We increase our responsibility
when we increase our sense of
accountability to God.*

Perfectionism

A friend visiting Auguste Rodin's studio towards the end of the sculptor's long and brilliant career, found him weeping over a statue he had just completed. He failed to understand the old man's grief, so looking at the statue the friend remarked: "But it is perfect!"

"I think so, too, and that is why I am in tears," explained Rodin. He had come to the moment of truth, the realisation that he had gone as far as his imagination and craftsmanship had taken him.

When he was at the very height of his fame, Montana's great artist Charles Russell was asked by a reporter just what he considered to be his greatest picture.

Russell thoughtfully considered the lengthy gallery of his magnificent scenes of the early West, then with characteristic humility, slowly answered: "I have not painted it yet."

In the same vein, when the famous architect Frank Lloyd Wright, at the age of 83, was asked which of his works he would select as his masterpiece, he replied, "My next one."

If you are satisfied with
yourself, you had better
change your ideals.

After he had completed his statue of Moses, a masterpiece, Michelangelo, full of fury, struck it and cried out, "Why do you not speak?"

The artist was clearly disappointed, not because his work lacked artistic perfection, but because he did not possess the divine powers of the Almighty Creator.

An eligible bachelor decided that he should have only the most perfect woman as his life partner. He looked around in his home town and finding none, decided to travel the world in search of one. After several years of wandering, he returned home tired and impoverished. A concerned neighbour asked him whether it was true that in spite of travelling through the most advanced cultures of the globe he had not come across a single perfect female.

"Well, to tell you the truth, I did find a perfect woman once."

"What happened then?"

"I asked her if she would marry me. She spent some time with me, then one day confessed that she wouldn't take me as her life partner. The reason she gave was simple: she was looking for a perfect man!"

She: The man I marry must be as brave as a lion, but not forward; handsome as Apollo, but not conceited; wise as Solomon, but meek as a lamb; a man who is kind to every woman, but loves only me.

He : How lucky we met.

✳   ✳   ✳

Sensitivity

Dr Leo Buscaglia, the renowned author, said that he was once asked to judge a contest to find the most caring child. The first prize was given to a four-year-old boy who showed very clearly that he had a caring attitude.

The wife of the elderly man who lived next door to the boy's house had recently died. Seeing the man in tears, the boy approached the man, climbed into his lap and just sat there. His mother later asked him what he had said to comfort the old man.

The boy replied, "Nothing. I just helped him to cry."

Once a young student of music visited the Beethoven museum in Bonn. She was fascinated by the piano on which Beethoven had composed some of his masterpieces. Giving a large tip to the museum guard, she requested him to allow her to play a few bars on it.

With tremendous excitement she sat down at the piano and played the opening bars of the *Moonlight Sonata*. On finishing, she said to the guard, "I suppose all the great pianists who visit this place want to play on that piano."

The guard shook his head. "Well, Paderewski was here a few years ago and he said he wasn't worthy to touch it."

A father once took his seven-year-old son to a pet shop. The shop owner showed them five beautiful pups. But the boy's eye fell on a pup lying in a nearby pen all by itself. He asked the owner about it. The owner explained that the pup was born with a bad leg — it was crippled, and he was going to end its life. The lad was suddenly moved to pity. "How can you do that?" he protested.

"Well," explained the owner, "you must realise that this puppy will never be able to run and play with a boy like you."

The boy whispered something into his father's ears, then told the owner that he would like to buy the handicapped pup.

"The charge is the same for this or for any other of the pups," said the owner. "Why don't you take a healthy one?"

In answer, the boy bent over and pulled up the pants on his right leg, exposing the brace underneath, and said, "Sir, I want this one because I understand what he's going through."

Malcolm Muggeridge tells us in *Something Beautiful for God* about the transformation he experienced in his sensitivity when accompanying Mother Teresa on his rounds at the Home for the Dying during his filming sessions.

He says he went through three phases. The first was horror mixed with pity, the second was compassion in its simple and pure forms; and the third, an awareness that the dying and derelict persons, the lepers, the unwanted children that he found there, were not objects of pity or repulsion, but rather "dear and delightful; as might be, friends of long standing, brothers and sisters."

✳   ✳   ✳

A teacher once gave his students an outdoor exercise to teach them a lesson in sensitivity. They were to go to some lonely pathways and find by the side of them a small, unnoticed flower. Then they must study, scrutinise the flower carefully, noticing the nuances of colours. They must observe how symmetrical the leaves were. The students went out and each found a flower and admired it. They brought their flower back with them.

After some feedback, the teacher told them how people, too, are like that flower. They have unique qualities and talents which may go waste and die if they are not noticed and appreciated by others.

In a public park in Exeter, England, there is a "Garden for the Blind." Easily accessible, though situated in a quiet corner, this garden is planted with shrubs, climbers, and flowers selected for their fragrance. The flower-beds and borders are elevated on grassy banks, enabling visitors to smell them without having to stoop.

A metal plaque, written in Braille, its raised dots worn bright from constant reading, bears the inscription. "To the blind of Exeter, with the thought that your main pleasure in a garden comes from the sweet scents to be found there, these plants have been selected for your enjoyment."

*Sympathy is the result of
thinking with your heart.*

A woman who had been suffering from "nerves" went to one of the best-known psychiatrists in town for treatment.

As she left the office after her first call, she turned and said, "Doctor, I know that I am highly sensitive."

"Madam," he answered, "I know that you are highly selfish."

The lady naturally left in something of a huff. But ten days later she returned and apologised. After a little reflection and prayer she said she had awakened to the fact that she was a thoroughly selfish woman.

In an orphanage there was a little girl who was greatly disliked by the warden and other staff members. They were all hoping that somehow she might be discovered by some distant relation and be taken away.

One day her dormitory supervisor observed the girl walk up to the gate, write a note, and tuck it in the branch of a tree standing nearby. She at once reported this to the warden. They got their hopes up. Perhaps she did have some contact outside, after all, either a friend or even a relative.

As soon as the girl was out of sight, the warden and the supervisor walked casually to the gate. They plucked out the crumpled note, opened it.

Written on it, in a child's scrawl, was this message: "Whoever finds this, I love you."

✳   ✳   ✳

Forgiveness

The short story called *Somebody's Son* by Richard Pindell, opens with David, a boy who has run away from home, sitting by the side of a road and writing a letter to his mother, in which he expresses the hope that his old-fashioned father will forgive him and accept him again as his son. Then he informs his mother: "In a few days I'll be passing our property. If dad will take me back, ask him to tie a white cloth on the apple tree in the field next to our home."

Days later David is on a train that will go past his house. He is nervous with suspense, wondering whether the white cloth will be there or not. As the train is about to arrive at the spot from which his house will be visible, David can't bring himself to look at it, so he turns to the man sitting next to him and says:

"Mister, will you do me a favour? Around this bend on the right, you'll see a tree. Tell me if there's a white cloth tied to it."

As the train rumbles past the tree, David stares straight ahead. Then, in a shaky voice he asks the man, "Mister, is a white cloth tied to one of the branches of the tree?"

The man answers in a surprised tone of voice: "Why, son, there's a white cloth tied to practically *every* branch."

> *Forgiveness is the fragrance that*
> *the trampled flower casts upon*
> *the heel that crushed it.*

In her book *Putting Forgiveness Into Practice*, Doris Donnelly describes an experience of reconciliation. A mother of three boys was abandoned by her husband and nearly went crazy.

One day, while driving the family car, with her three sons in the back seat, she suddenly spun around in a fit of anger, slapped her seven-year-old across the face, and yelled at him, saying that she gave him birth only because she wanted his father to remain with her, but now he was gone. "I hate you," she told the boy.

This incident left a deep wound in the boy's heart. The wound was kept fresh with his mother constantly finding fault with him and treating him badly.

However, at the age of 30, away from home, his attitudes changed drastically. He began to review the ugly incident from his mother's point of view. He realised she was in a bad way then: young, penniless, jobless, and with a family to support. Obviously, she felt anger, pain, frustration.

One day the young man visited his mother and told her that he understood her feelings and that he loved her in spite of everything. Son and mother embraced each other; and as they clung together, they both wept unashamedly. That was the beginning of a new relationship.

> *It has been rightly said that*
> *forgiveness is the quality of*
> *heart that forgets the injury,*
> *reconciles with the offender.*

As a schoolboy, the English author C.S. Lewis was often victimised by a teacher. He felt deeply hurt, and carried a scar for most of his life. Every now and again he would feel the sting, and give in to unpleasant thoughts about the teacher.

As Lewis matured, he realised that the wound would heal only if he forgave the teacher from his heart. He tried hard to reconcile himself to what had happened in childhood, yet he just could not get himself to forgive the wrong done to him. To make matters worse, he suffered from severe guilt-feelings because of his inability to forgive.

Finally, shortly before his death, Lewis wrote to a friend: "Only a few weeks ago, I suddenly realised that I had at last forgiven the schoolmaster who so darkened my childhood. I'd been trying to do it for years and each time I thought I'd done it, I found it had to be attempted again. But this time, I feel sure it is the real thing."

A friend of Clara Barton's, founder of the American Red Cross, once reminded her of an especially cruel thing that had been done to her many years before. But Miss Barton seemed not to recall it. "Don't you remember it?" her friend asked.

"No," came the reply. "I distinctly remember forgetting that."

The trouble with people
forgiving and forgetting is
that they keep reminding us
they're doing it.

There is a legend about Leonardo da Vinci of the time when he was painting *The Last Supper*. One day he is said to have had a big quarrel with someone. Afterward, he went to his studio and began to paint the face of Jesus. But he found, to his utter dismay, that there was a strange feeling in his hand, and it became impossible to use the brush with any effect. He immediately left the place, went to the man he had fought with, and asked his forgiveness.

When he returned to the studio and resumed painting the face of Jesus, he was his normal self again.

There is a parable by E.V. Lucas. It tells of a woman who, upon receiving news from the war office that her soldier son had been killed in battle, kept repeating deliriously: "Oh that I might see him again, if only for five minutes — but to see him."

An angel answered her prayer. He asked: Which five minutes in the life of her 30-year-old son would she like to see? Would she like to see him as a soldier dying heroically at his post? Or, as a boy, when he stepped on stage to receive the highest honours in school? Or, as a babe at her breast?

After a brief silence the mother replied: "No, I would have him for five minutes as he was one day when he ran in from the garden to ask my forgiveness for being naughty. He was so small and so unhappy, and he flew into my arms with such force that he hurt me."

> *When someone does a wrong,*
> *don't rub it in; rub it out.*

A man who was in a lift saw a woman rushing toward it and so he held the door back for her. She jumped in, thanked him, and explained that she was late for work because she had overslept.

"You need not worry about it," said the man in an attempt to reassure her. "God will certainly forgive you."

"No doubt He will," said the stressed woman, "but the sad fact is that I don't work for *Him*."

Arthur Pinero, the famous dramatist, once said, "If you have anything to pardon, pardon quickly. Slow forgiveness is little better than no forgiveness."

Once while talking about family matters, a man remarked to his friend: "I must tell you something. Whenever me and my wife begin an argument, she get *historical*."

"You mean hysterical, don't you?"

"No, I mean historical," persisted the man."She remembers everything I ever did wrong and exactly where and when it happened."

> *To say one can forgive but*
> *cannot forget is only*
> *another way of saying one*
> *cannot forgive.*

Modesty

When the famous physician, Sir William Osler, would make the grand rounds of the hospital, he would be accompanied by a number of admiring interns. He would stop at the beds of patients and examine them carefully. Every now and then, however, after checking the sick person, he would scribble the initials "G.O.K." on the chart.

One day a student made bold to ask the distinguished doctor what the words G.O.K. stood for.

Osler, with a smile and a shrug, replied, "God Only Knows."

There is a story told of a philosopher in ancient China who enjoyed the patronage of the Emperor himself. He was a humble person, and whenever he was asked a question he had no answer for, he would reply, "I do not know."

Once somebody, upset with this show of ignorance, confronted him: "But the Emperor pays you for what you know."

"That's true," replied the philosopher patiently. "If he paid me for what I did not know, not only the wealth of the empire but of the entire world would not suffice."

The more a person knows,
the more is he inclined
to be modest.

Sir Isaac Newton confessed: "I do not know what I may appear to the world, but to myself I seem to have been only like a boy playing on the seashore and diverting myself in now and then finding a smoother pebble or a prettier shell than ordinary, whilst the great ocean of truth lay all undiscovered before me."

A certain cardinal was once called upon to give evidence in a court case, and to impress the jury, the defense counsel asked if he was the leader of the Catholics.

"That's right," said the cardinal.

"In fact, you are a Prince of the Church of Rome?"

"Correct."

"One of the greatest scholars not only in this country but also in the world?"

"True."

"A brilliant man in every way?"

"Yes, of course."

Later a friend reproached the cardinal, "You weren't very humble today, were you?"

The cardinal smiled, "True," he said, "but what could I do? I was on oath."

The greater a person's talent, the more becoming his modesty.

During a rehearsal of Beethoven's Ninth Symphony, the members of the orchestra were so overwhelmingly moved by the conducting of Arturo Toscanini that they rose as one man and applauded him. When the spontaneous cheering had subsided Toscanini turned to his men, tears glistening in his eyes.

"Please... please! Don't do this!" he said in a pathetic voice. "You see, gentlemen, it isn't me you should applaud. It's Beethoven!"

A celebrated French artist who never bothered much with his appearance was out walking one morning when he heard a feminine voice behind him call: "My good man, can you carry my bundle a little way for me?"

Turning, he saw a very beautiful woman; so instead of explaining who he was, he said, "Most willingly, madame," and took the bundle from her.

First into one shop then into another he followed her. Finally the woman came to her home and fumbled in her purse for some change. But when she offered it to him, the artist refused.

"Madame," he said, "I am not a porter, despite the ungracious compliment you paid my appearance. I am an artist, and I shall be well repaid if I can make a copy of your beautiful face and send it to the next exhibition at the Academy."

A modest person is generally
admired — if people ever
hear of him.

Humility

Mahatma Gandhi always sought to identify himself with the poor of India, by living as simple and humble a life as possible. He avoided all forms of luxury and ostentation.

Once he was asked why he always travelled by third class in railway trains. "Because there is no fourth class," he replied.

Paul Cezanne never knew that he was later to be considered 'the father of modern painting'. Because of his great love for his work, he never thought of recognition. He struggled for thirty-five years, living in oblivion at Aix, giving away masterpieces to indifferent neighbours.

And then one day a discerning Paris dealer happened upon his canvases and, gathering several of them, presented the first Cezanne exhibit. The great of the art world were stunned: here, indeed, was a Master!

And Cezanne himself was no less astonished. Arriving at the gallery on the arm of his son, he gazed wonderingly at his paintings, and tears came to his eyes.

"Look," he whispered. "They've framed them!"

Sincere humility attracts.
Lack of humility subtracts.
Artificial humility detracts.

The radio genius, Marconi, once spent practically the whole night with a friend, discussing the most intricate phases of wireless communication. When his friend was about to leave, Marconi suddenly remarked:

"All my life I have been studying this phenomenon, but there is one thing I simply cannot understand about radio."

His friend turned to him in disbelief and asked: "What is that?"

"Why does it work?" replied Marconi quietly.

Some years ago a raw army recruit was tending a lawn in the Camp area when a man in uniform passed by.

"Hey, buddy, let's have a match," the recruit called out. Silently the man obliged.

When the passer-by was out of earshot, another soldier took the rookie to task. "Do you know who that was?" he roared. "That was General Pershing!"

Shocked, the rookie set off to apologise.

"I'm sorry, sir," he stammered, when he caught up with the general. "I've only been in the Army a couple of hours and all uniforms look alike to me. I hope you won't —"

"That's all right, son," Pershing smiled. Then, patting the rookie on the shoulder, he continued, "But take my advice and never try it on a second lieutenant."

> *To be humble to superiors is*
> *duty; to equals, courtesy,*
> *to inferiors, nobility.*

Humour

A bald-headed man was celebrating his birthday. In order to tease him, a friend presented him with a comb, and waited for his reaction when he opened the gift.

"Thanks," said the bald man without batting an eyelid. "I'll never part with it!"

Adlai Stevenson used to make public speeches during his campaign tours in the fight for presidency against General Dwight D. Eisenhower. On one occasion the chairman of the assembly introduced him in a flowery fashion.

Stevenson began his speech by saying: "After hearing what the chairman has said, I can hardly wait to hear myself speak."

When Thomas More was about to be hanged he requested the executioner to help him climb the stairs of the execution platform. "See me safe up. For my coming down I can shift for myself."

And he is said to have added, "And let us pray for each other so that we will meet merrily in heaven."

*A sense of humour can help
you overlook the unattractive,
tolerate the unpleasant, cope
with the unexpected, and smile
through the unbearable.*

A person with a keen sense of humour was hospitalised for some minor ailment. He was advised rest and told to take certain medicines. The following day, when he dropped in on his round, the doctor was happy to see the patient moving quite cheerfully.

"You look much better," said the doctor. And pointing to the medicine bottle asked, "Have you been following the instructions on it?"

"Of course," replied the patient. "I've kept the bottle tightly closed."

Manager: "I can't do a thing with Balan. I've had him in three departments, and he dozes all day."

Proprietor: "Put him at the pyjamas counter, and fasten a card on him with the words: Our pyjamas are of such superior quality that even the man who sells them cannot keep awake."

Once, on a visit to Pope John XXIII, a diplomat asked the pontiff: "How many people work in the Vatican City, Holy Father?"

"About half," said the Pope with a smile.

> *Genuine humour is always kindly*
> *and gracious. It points out the*
> *weakness of humanity, but shows*
> *no contempt and leaves no sting.*

The American humorist, Gelett Burghes, attended a lecture in Paris one evening. The speaker began by asking everyone to laugh. Someone snickered. Another chuckled. And then, urged on by the speaker, someone laughed. Others joined in and before long the entire audience was laughing uproariously.

Burgess wasn't in a mood for laughing when he went to the lecture. Fact is, he was going through a troubled period in his life. He hadn't even smiled for some time. But the laughter was contagious and, before he knew it, he was laughing with the rest. At the end of the evening he was feeling better.

The next day he picked up a magazine and saw the laughing face of a woman who had won lottery winner. She was delighted with her good fortune and it showed. Burgess pinned the picture on a wall and every time he looked at it, he had to smile.

That gave him an idea. He began collecting pictures of people laughing. He found them in newspapers, advertisements, and magazines, and soon he had a scrapbook filled with people radiating happiness.

One day he showed it to a nurse. She threw back her head and laughed until tears rolled down her cheeks. The nurse took the scrapbook to a hospital and showed it to a patient. The patient smiled for the first time in months. Soon the scrapbook was being sent from bed to bed, and from ward to ward, and everyone felt the better for it.

When comedian George Burns was asked about his title role in the film *Oh, God*, the 82-year-old star explained, "It wasn't hard to play God. At my age, everything I do is a miracle."

✳   ✳   ✳

Approaches

There is a legend about three men who each carried two sacks, one in front and one behind.

When asked what were in his sacks, the first man answered: "The sack on my back contains all the kind deeds done to me by my friends; the one in front is filled with the unkind deeds done to me." It was found that the man made very little progress on the way.

The second man was questioned about the contents of his sacks. "The sack in front contains my good deeds," he explained. "I occasionally take them out and air them. Behind me I carry a sack full of my mistakes; and it's a heavy one, indeed." This man too, did not make much progress.

When the third man was asked about his sacks, he replied. "The front sack is full of the kind deeds of my friends; I like pulling them out and showing them to others. Though the sack is full," explained the man, "it is not as heavy as it seems; in fact, to me it acts as a sail in the wind, pushing me ahead."

"And what about that empty sack on your back?" he was asked.

"Oh that," he said, "you see, I made a hole at the bottom of it. I throw into it all the insults, the negative remarks, and the misdeeds of people. They slip out through the hole and don't impede my progress."

> *Take a constructive approach*
> *to personal feedback. If it's*
> *untrue, disregard it; if it's*
> *unfair, keep from irritation;*
> *if it's ignorant, smile; if it's*
> *justified, learn from it.*

D. DIMENSIONS OF PERSONALITY

The humane aspects

Magnanimity

There was a young married couple very wealthy but childless. They decided to adopt two orphans. They visited an orphanage and were treated as royalty.

The officials asked them to fill out the necessary forms. That done, the superintendent of the irstitution, beaming with satisfaction, said, "Now let's go and I will present you with two of the nicest children of the home."

The wife turned quickly and remarked kindly but firmly, "Oh, please do not! We are not interested in the nicest children. Give us the two that nobody else would take!"

Appreciation

Nathanael Hawthorne was feeling desperate when he lost his job at the customs-house. But his wife, Sofia, surprised him by saying with a smile, "Now you can write your book."

Nathanael asked her in bitter tones what they would survive on if he did so.

In response Sofia pulled out a bundle of cash which she had been saving in secret in a drawer. "I have always known that you were a man of genius," she explained. "I knew that some day you would write an immortal masterpiece. So every week, out of the money you gave me for house-keeping, I have saved something. Here is enough to last us one whole year."

✳   ✳   ✳

Trust

Tamara Andreas, in *Core Transformation*, tells of an experience she
had one day when travelling in a bus. A father and mother, both
clearly blind, boarded the bus with a boy and a girl. The couple
and the children settled down in seats across from each other.

During the journey, the father said nervously, "Nancy! Danny! What
are you doing? Are you sitting down while the bus is moving?" He
was flustered and agitated. The mother rubbed her husband's knee
with one hand and responded, in a calm, clear voice, "The children
are doing fine." Her manner and presence exuded a sense of deep
inner peacefulness that allowed her to trust her small children even
though she could not see them.

In his book *Eage of Adventure*, Bruce Larson tells the story about a
letter found in a baking-powder tin wired to the handle of an old
pump, which offered the only hope of drinking water on a very
long and seldom-used trail across the Amargosa Desert in the USA.
The letter read as follows:

"This pump is alright as of June 1932. I put the new leather sucker
washer into it, and it ought to last several years. But this leather
washer dries out and the pump has got to be primed. Under the white
rock, I buried a bottle of water. There's enough water in it to prime
the pump, but not if you drink some first. Pour in about one-quarter,
and let her soak to wet the leather. Then pour in the rest, medium
fast and pump like crazy. You'll get water. The well has never run
dry. Have faith. When you get watered up, fill the bottle and put it
back like you found it for the next feller. (Signed) Desert Pete.

P.S. Don't go drinking up the water first. Prime the pump with it
first, and you'll get all you can hold."

Gratitude

There is an incident regarding Mother Teresa described in B.K.R. Pai's *Mother of Love*. Mother saw a woman lying in the gutter of a Calcutta lane. She was being eaten away by worms, disease-ridden and unconscious. Mother took her to her home for the destitutes, gave her a bath and put her in bed. Afterwards, Mother touched her hand to soothe her. The woman's face for a few fleeting moments lit up with a serene smile and she said, "Thank you." And then she died.

"If I were in her position," concluded Mother Teresa, "I would have said: I'm hungry, I'm sick. I would never have said: Thank you. It is the woman who taught me a lesson of gratitude."

British columnist Bernard Levin, commenting on the attitude of two music critics: "If this pair had been present at the miracle of the loaves and fishes, one of them would have complained that there was no lemon to go with the fish, and the other would have demanded butter for the bread."

Courtesy

At an air-conditioned shopping centre, a distinguished looking grey-haired man and a pretty young woman arrived at the door at the same time. The man spontaneously reached out for the handle and held the door open for her.

She said, "Don't hold the door for me just because I'm a lady."

The man was taken aback. After a moment's silence he said: "I didn't open the door because you are a lady. I opened it because I'm a gentleman."

*   *   *

Generosity

Frank O'Connor in *An Only Child*, recalls a childhood incident. One Christmas, Santa Claus had brought him a toy engine. Later in the day, when he visited a crib in a convent, he was distressed on seeing the little Infant without toys, whereas he at least had something.

He asked the nuns if Jesus did not like toys, and was told that He did, but His mother was too poor to afford Him any. Frank knew that his mother, too, was poor, but at Christmas she always managed to buy him something, even if it was only a box of crayons.

Frank said that he distinctly remembers getting into the crib and putting the engine between the outstretched arms of Jesus. He probably showed the babe how to wind it as well, or how else would the Child manage.

He remembers too "the tearful feeling of reckless generosity" with which he left the Infant there in the nightly darkness of the chapel, clutching the toy engine to his chest.

✳

Nikos Kazantzakis, the well-known Greek writer, describes an experience he had while visiting the island of Crete. One day, while he was out walking, he saw an elderly woman carrying a basket of figs. As she passed by him, she laid down the basket, picked out two beautiful figs and presented them to the author. Nikos asked her, "Do you know me, old lady?"

She looked at him in amazement. "No, my boy. Do I have to know you to give you something? You are a human being, are you not? So am I. Isn't that enough?"

> *Generosity will always leave*
> *pleasant memories.*

Convictions

A patrician once sought the help of the philosopher Epictetus. "Nero commands me to play the buffoon in the arena," said the elder. "This is a serious matter of self-respect for me. What would you do in my place?"

Epictetus answered, "In your place I would obey Nero."

"What! You would play the buffoon in the arena?"

"No," said the philosopher, "*I* would not. But you may as well do, since you are willing to discuss the matter."

An old pilgrim was on his way to a temple situated on a high peak in the Himalayas. Since it began to snow, he stopped at an inn. When the innkeeper found out that the man, with wrinkled features and lean physique, was headed for the temple, he said incredulously, "How will you ever get to the temple in this weather?"

The old pilgrim answered cheerfully, "My heart has already got there; now it's easy for the rest of me to follow."

A prominent executive was once asked what her formula for success was. "It's very simple," she replied. "Just ten simple two-letter words: *If it is to be, it is up to me.*"

✳   ✳   ✳

Endurance

Persistence

"You ought to feel highly honoured, young man," said the Chief Minister to the reporter. "Do you know, I have refused to see seven reporters today?"

"Yes, sir, I know," said the reporter. "I was them."

Florist: "Take a bunch of flowers home for your wife, sir."

Man on the street: "I haven't got a wife."

Florist: "Then buy a bunch for your sweetheart."

Man : "I don't have a sweetheart, either."

Florist : "Well, then, buy a couple of bunches to celebrate your good fortune."

Disciple: "Sir, what is the difference between perseverance and obstinacy?"

Master: "One is a strong will and the other is a strong won't."

✳   ✳   ✳

There is a book, popular in business circles, by Laurence J. Peter, entitled *The Peter Principle: Why things Always Go Wrong*. When Peter first sent his manuscript to McGraw Hill, he got a rejection letter from the publications editor which stated: "I can foresee no commercial possibilities for such a book and consequently can offer no encouragement."

Undeterred, Peter sent his manuscript to another well-known publisher, and yet another, only to have it sent back. In all, 30 publishers rejected it, because they found that it had limited market value. But Peter did not give up. He contacted William Morrow and Company, who did accept it. And the book sold over 8 million copies!

During World War II a transport plane crashed in the Pacific, and the lives of thirty-three people were at stake. Rescue planes scoured the area of the crash in vain. According to reports, one of the rescue planes was commanded by a certain Lieut. Commander Steve Kora.

He was about to give up the search when a member of his crew urged him to give it just one more try. "It's only a matter of eight minutes," he pleaded.

The pilot agreed. In less than five minutes they sighted the victims clinging to life-rafts and rescued them all.

Thirty-three men owed their lives to that one man who said, "Let's try again."

Persistence prevails
when all else fails.

Persuasion

The great pianist Arthur Rubinstein never signed autographs. Once, however, he was confronted by a teenager after a concert. The youngster held out a pad and pencil and said, "I know your fingers are tired, sir, but mine are, too, from clapping."

Rubinstein obliged.

Patience

"What is your formula for success?" asked the young man of the successful financier.

"Patience, my lad," said the old man. "Anything in the world can be accomplished if one only has patience."

"I'll wager I can name one thing that cannot be done, even with the utmost patience," said the young man.

"And what's that?"

"Carrying water in a sieve," answered the youth.

"Even that can be done," was the reply. "If one will only have the patience to wait until it freezes."

The great Polish pianist and composer, Ignace Jan Paderewski, renowned for the virtuosity of his playing, was once asked by an admirer how he had reached such a state of perfection in his field. It must have involved a lot of patience, the admirer remarked.

"Everyone has patience," said Paderewski. "I learned to use mine."

*   *   *

Constructive

I watched them tearing a building down,
    a gang of men in a busy town.
With a ho-heave-ho and a lusty yell
    they swung a beam and the sidewall fell.
I asked the foreman, "Are these men skilled,
    and the men you'd hire if you had to build?"

He gave a laugh, said "No, indeed;
    just common labour is all I need.
I can easily wreck in a day or two
    what builders have taken a year to do."

I thought to myself as I went my way,
    which of these roles have I tried to play?
Am I a builder who works with care,
    measuring life by the rule and the square?
Am I shaping my deed to a well-made plan,
    patiently doing the best I can?
Or am I a wrecker, who walks the town,
    content with the labour of tearing down?

Driving into a town after a weekend at the lake, a couple encountered a dismal, foggy, drizzly morning.

"This day isn't going to be worth anything," said the wife. "It's a good-for-nothing day."

"Well," replied her husband, "It's holding yesterday and tomorrow together."

✳ ✳ ✳

Impact

One fine day St Francis of Assisi invited a young monk to
accompany him to the town to preach. They set out, wandering
through the main streets of the town. Several people turned to them
with a friendly word of greeting. They returned the greeting with a
nod, a smile, or words of cheer.

Every now and then they would stop to caress a child or speak to
someone. And all along the way St Francis and the monk carried
on a lively conversation between them. After they had rambled
quite a distance, the young monk grew anxious and asked St Francis
when and where they were going to begin their preaching.

"We have been preaching from the time we left the monastery door,"
replied the saint. "Haven't people been observing our joyfulness,
or feeling inspired by our greetings and smiles; haven't they noticed
how pleasantly we behave towards each other along the way? If
these are not all little sermons, what are they?"

Disciple: Tell me the difference between one who preaches and one
who practises.

Master: Those who preach use a torch to show the way; those who
practise are the torch.

> *Some of the best preaching is
> done by holding the tongue.*

Alert

Abul Khair, a nine-year-old boy who lived in the eastern Bangladesh farming village of Toragar, awoke as usual at dawn on July 13, 1996. Crossing the rail-road line on his way to a canal, where he gathered snails to feed his ducks, he noticed a break in the rails. He realised he was looking at a potential calamity. The crowded morning Express from Chandpur to Chittagong was due at any moment, and if he did not warn the crew in time, the train would derail.

After rousing residents of a nearby fish farm to alert them to the danger, Abul raced home, snatched a red undergarment of his grandmother's and ran back to the railroad. With the whistle of the approaching train in his ears, Abul clambered onto a railroad bridge near the broken section and frantically waved the red cloth.

The driver slammed on the brakes, bringing the train to a grinding halt just short of the breach. The sudden stop was the first the 1,000 passengers knew of their close brush with death.

A Dominican, a Franciscan, and a Jesuit were meeting in a room. In the middle of their discussion the light went out. Undeterred by the darkness, the Dominican stood up and said, "Let us consider the nature of light and darkness, and their meaning." The Franciscan began to sing a hymn in honour of "Our Little Sister Darkness."

The Jesuit went out and replaced the fuse.

✳   ✳   ✳

Involved

A researcher once wanted to try out an experiment. He hired a man who could chop wood, took him to his backyard, and handing him an axe, gave the following instruction:

"Do you see that log lying there? Well, I want you to go through the motions of chopping it — only you must use the reverse side of the axe, not the blade. I'll pay you a hundred rupees for the job."

The man thought the researcher was crazy, but he was paying well, so why not do as he says? He began work immediately. A couple of hours later, the man presented himself to the researcher. "Mister," he said, "I would like to quit the job."

"What's the matter" Do you feel the pay's too little? Well, I'll double it for you."

"You won't understand," replied the man. "The pay is fine. But when I chop wood I've got to see the chips fly!"

Foreman: "I'll bet you're one of those people that drop their work and beat it as soon as the whistle blows."

Worker: "Not me. After I quit work I usually wait about five minutes for the whistle to blow."

The plain fact is that human beings are happy only when they are striving for something worthwhile.

E. SPOTTED IDENTITIES

Cautious

When he was well on in years, the famed pianist Arthur Rubinstein was asked by an interviewer: "Am I right in thinking that you're playing better now than every before?"
"I think so," he answered.
"Is it experience, practice, what?"
"No, no, no," said Rubinstein. "I am 80. So now I take chances I never took before. You see, the stakes are not so high. I can afford it. I used to be so much more careful — no wrong notes, not too bold ideas, watch tempi. Now I let go and enjoy myself, and to hell with everything except the music."

When the municipal clerk of a certain town in Western Europe went on a vacation, he left the following sign prominently displayed on his office door:

For registration of births and deaths see Dr Barr. For auto and truck licences, to Saint Rose. For municipal business, see Mr Fletch. For marriage licenses — think it over carefully and come back again in ten days.

✸

It was said of a manager: "John is so cautious in everything that he looks left and right before crossing a cheque."

Caution is a good risk to take.

Calculating

A person was entertaining a guest at his house. During the meal the guest said: "I think that's enough. I've eaten seven slices of bread. So no more."

The host said: "Seven? You have taken eleven, but who's counting?"

Self-assumption

Tom Selleck, the noted film actor, has this confession to make: Whenever I get full of myself, I remember the nice, elderly couple who approached me with a camera on a street in Honolulu one day. When I struck a pose for them, the man said, "No, no, we want *you* to take a picture of *us*."

A celebrated surgeon, booked with patients months in advance, was no respecter of persons. Once the President's daughter came to his office, and he told her casually to take a seat. The lady was shocked. Was it possible the doctor didn't know who she was?

"I am the President's daughter," she said.

"Well!" the surgeon replied, "Take two seats."

> *If I saw myself as*
> *other people see me, would*
> *I need an introduction?*

Father: "And there, my son, I've told you the story of your daddy and the Great World War."

Son: "Yes, daddy, but what did they need all the other soldiers for?"

False humility

Two men went to a church to pray, a priest and his watchman. The priest began to beat his breast and, carried away, cried out, "I am the lowliest of men, Lord, unworthy of your grace! I am a void, a nothing; have mercy on me."

Within hearing distance of the priest knelt the watchman. He too, out of emotion, beat his breast and cried, "O Lord, have pity on me. I'm a sinner. I'm a nothing before your eyes."

The priest turned round haughtily. "Ha!" he said. "Look who's claiming to be nothing!"

Conceit

A conceited young clergyman delivered a sermon and sought his bishop's opinion of it.

"Well," said the bishop, "since you ask me, I think your sermon resembled the great sword of Charlemagne."

"It was a victorious sword, was it not?" replied the young man, deeply flattered.

"Yes," said the bishop, "it was. But it was also long and flat."

Conceit is a form of "I"
strain that doctors can't cure.

Ingratitude

A young mother took her four-year-old daughter to the market one day, and they strolled through stalls filled with colourful fruits and vegetables. When they stopped at a stall, the little girl stared at a neat pyramid of plump oranges before her. The proprietor came around and presented her with an orange.

The wide-eyed child looked at the orange, then at the man, again at the orange, again at the man.

Then her mother said, "What do you say to the nice man, dear?"

The little girl held up the orange to the man and said, "Peel it!"

We can assume this was not the answer the mother expected.

Infallibility

After carefully checking the patient the doctor said, "You have had an attack of pneumonia. You are some sort of musician, aren't you?"

"Yes," said the man surprised.

"And you play a wind instrument."

"That's right. How did you know?"

"Elementary, my dear fellow! There is a distinct straining of the lungs and the larynx is inflamed, undoubtedly because of severe pressure. Tell me, what instrument do you play?"

"The accordion."

✳   ✳   ✳

Presumption

A woman went to her car one morning and found that the radio had been stolen. It was easy to see how the thief had got in — there was a gaping void where the side window should have been.

Deciding the first priority was to have the window replaced, she left the car at the garage for repairs, after an uncomfortable drive in the cold weather.

When she returned that evening, somewhat nervous about the bill, she was told there was no charge.

The window was not damaged, the garage man explained. It had been wound down.

There was a new employee at a large office who stood before the paper shredder looking utterly confused.

A secretary passing by asked, "Need some help?"

"Yes," he replied, "how does this thing work?"

"Simple," she said, taking the thick-sized report from his hand and feeding it into the shredder.

"Thanks," he said, "but where do the copies come out?"

> *The person who knows every-*
> *thing has a lot to learn.*

There is an ancient tale about a king who wanted to pick the wisest man among his subjects to be his prime minister. When the search finally narrowed down to just three men, he decided to put them to the supreme test.

Accordingly, he placed them together in a room in his palace, and on the room door he had installed a lock which was the last word in mechanical ingenuity. The candidates were informed that whoever was able to open the door first would be appointed to the post of honour.

The three men immediately set themselves to the task. Two of them began at once to work out complicated mathematical formulas to discover the proper lock combination.

The third man, however, just sat down in his chair, lost in thought. Finally, without bothering to put pen to paper, he got up, walked to the door, and turned the handle. And the door opened to his touch.

It had been unlocked all the time.

Voice on the telephone: "Is my husband in the Club?"

Club receptionist: "No, madam, I'm afraid he isn't."

Voice: "But how do you know? I didn't tell you my name."

Receptionist: "Husbands are never here, madam — especially those who are wanted on the phone."

✳   ✳   ✳

At one session of a personality workshop, the instructor gave the participants an exercise. He asked them to write down the length of the hall they were in.

Every one answered with round figures, like fifty feet, sixty feet, and so on. Some added the word 'approximately'. At the end of the exercise, the instructor said, "Not a single one of you has given the correct answer."

"What is it?" asked the participants.

"The correct answer is, I DO NOT KNOW," said the instructor.

Low self-reliance

A blind man visited a friend and when it came time to leave it was already dark. His friend offered him a lantern. He was amused.

"What good would it do me," he said, "day and night are the same to me."

But his friend persisted. "Carry it anyway, so that people will not bump into you."

The blind man left, and it wasn't long before someone knocked him off balance, shouting, "Why don't you look where you are going?"

The blind man replied, "Can't you see this lantern?"

"Sorry, brother," the stranger said, "but your lantern has gone out."

✳ ✳ ✳

Apathy

They do not lie; they just neglect to tell the truth.

They do not take; they simply cannot bring themselves to give.

They do not steal; they scavenge.

They will not rock the boat; but did you ever see them pull an oar?

They will not pull you down; they'll simply let you pull them up, and let that pull you down.

They do not hurt you; they merely will not help you.

They do not hate you; they merely cannot love you.

They will not burn you; they'll only fiddle while you burn.

They are the nothing people; the sins-of-omission folk; the neither-good-nor-bad-and-therefore-worse. Because the good at least keep busy trying, and the bad try just as hard. Both have that character that comes from caring, action, and conviction. These have nothing.

> He's a real Nowhere Man,
> Sitting in his Nowhere Land,
> Making all his Nowhere plans for Nobody.
> Doesn't have a point of view,
> Knows not where he's going to,
> Isn't he a bit like you and me?
>
> *Beatles*

✳   ✳   ✳

False priorities

Outside the Race Course at Mahalakhsmi, in Mumbai, a shady-looking character accosted a rich business man, and pleaded: "Could you give me Rs 50? I haven't eaten in two days."

"How do I know you won't use it to gamble," asked the business man.

"No way," replied the scum. "I already have my gambling money."

In *The Wife of Pilate*, Gertrude von le Fort has imaginatively recreated the terror and panic that grips Claudia, the wife of Pilate, when she awakens from a dream in which she has seen future generations of people all praying the words of the creed: "suffered under Pontius Pilate."

She is so shocked by what the dream seems to forebode that she sends an urgent warning to her husband: "Have nothing to do with that innocent man."

But Pilate is guided by selfish priorities. Though convinced that Jesus is innocent, Pilate yields to mob-pressure. He condemns Jesus to the most brutal form of Roman execution — crucifixion, then attempts to purge himself of guilt by the ritual washing of his hands.

✳   ✳   ✳

F. PSYCHOLOGICAL DISORDERS

Isolation

In his book *Life Is Tremendous*, Charles E. Jones makes the distinction between "I-Land" and "You-Land".

He says the I-Land is a lonely place, and countless thousands are shipwrecked on its shores after setting their sails away from You-Land. Perhaps they merely drift into I-Land, but the result is the same: loneliness and slow death for people who never experience the thrill of learning to live.

Self-righteousness

A newspaper editor was stubborn and hard-headed. One day an indignant reporter said to him, "You always think you're right. But I'm sure you have realised that at times you are wrong."

"Yes," replied the editor, "I can recall one instance when I was wrong."

"I'm glad you admit it," the reporter shouted. "When was it?"

"Oh, it happened some time ago," said the editor, "when I thought I was wrong and I wasn't."

> *Anybody who tells you he*
> *never made a mistake in*
> *his life is probably*
> *relying on a poor memory*
> *— his or yours.*

Blind spots

At an army camp, the company commander was making the usual rounds of inspections when he came across a recruit whose pocket was unbuttoned.

Commander: "Button that pocket!"

Recruit: "Now, sir?"

Commander: "Right now."

So the recruit obediently reached up and fastened the Commander's unbuttoned pocket.

A cartoonist was once at a party with a group of close friends. Someone suggested that he draw a quick caricature of each person present. He obliged. When he completed the task, he passed the sketches around for everyone to look at. There was loud laughter and joking. But soon everyone realised that something strange was happening. While each one could recognise the others instantly, few could recognise themselves at first glance.

A timid first-year student said: "Excuse me, professor, but I couldn't make out what you wrote in the margin of my last paper."

The professor, glaring back at the young student replied: "I simply told you to write in clear handwriting."

✳   ✳   ✳

An airline was conducting a training flight for new personnel. During take-off the trainee flight engineer noticed suddenly that one of the engines was on fire. With a wrench he had in his hand, he touched the pilot's shoulder and said, "We're on fire!"

The pilot soon had the plane safely back on the ground. The engineer was explaining to the ground crew how calmly he had spotted the trouble, how he had called the pilot's attention to it without panic or excitement.

As he was talking, he saw the pilot being carried from the plane on a stretcher. "What's the matter with him?" asked the trainee engineer.

"Broken shoulder," replied the medic.

A woman said to her husband at a cocktail party, "George, you must not drink any more."

"Why not?" asked the surprised husband. "I'm perfectly sober."

"No, you are not," said the wife. "Your face is beginning to look blurred already."

*

When a husband found his wife unbearably domineering, he persuaded her to visit a psychiatrist. His wife had an hour-long session with the doctor, during which he waited outside. When she emerged, he asked her whether she had made any progress.

"Not much," she replied. "It took me fifty minutes to convince that man that his couch would look better against the wall."

*   *

Absent - mindedness

Once a professor rushed to the University's library counter in distress. He asked if he could find out who had borrowed a particular book, as he needed it that day. The new librarian, eager to please, immediately rifled through the file. "I've found it," she declared, "Professor Fernandes has it."

"Have I?" said the professor, looking confused and slightly embarrassed. "I'll have to go and look for it, then."

*

Servant: "The doctor is here, Professor."

Absent-minded professor: "Dear me! I'm in bed. I can't see him. Er... tell him I'm ill."

*

"I have brought a frog," said the zoology professor to his attentive students, "fresh from the pond, for dissection." He carefully unwrapped the package he carried and inside was a neatly prepared sandwich. The good professor looked at it with astonishment.

"Odd!" he said, "I distinctly remember having eaten my lunch."

G. K. Chesterton was once travelling, when athe train conductor asked for his ticket. He searched his pockets frantically. The conductor told him not to worry, he trusted he had it. "I know I have it," Chesterton stammered. "But what I want to know is, where in the world am I going?"

Rationalisation

There was a person who often used the old saying: *Don't leave for tomorrow what you can do today*. One day, though there were several urgent matters to attend to, he decided to take the afternoon off. A colleague caught him sneaking out of the office and challenged : "What about the motto you preach to others? Have you forgotten it?"

"Oh, no," he replied. "But no one can assure me that tomorrow I'll have some free time to relax."

A chronic late-comer at the office was confronted by the boss: "This is unforgivable. I've been repeatedly warning you about punctuality, and you keep on coming late. What I don't understand is, why, in spite of your living just a couple of streets away, you cannot be on time, whereas the clerk who lives three miles away is always on time."

"Well, it is like this, sir. The man who stays quite some distance away can make haste if he's late, and cover up lost time. He can take a cab if he misses the bus. But since I'm so near, there's no way I can hurry. If I'm late, I'm late."

✳

You have two chances: one of getting the germ and one of not. If you get the germ, you have two chances: one of getting the disease and one of not. It you get the disease, you have two chances: one of dying and one of not. And if you die — well, you still have two chances!

✳　✳　✳

On his eighth birthday, a boy held out a plate with two pieces of cake on it to his sister. She immediately grabbed the bigger piece. The boy protested: "That's not fair. Where are your manners? If you had given me the choice, I would have taken the smaller slice."

"Well," replied the sister triumphantly, "that's what you've got, so what's the complaint?"

Isn't it funny, when the other fellow takes a long time to do something, he's slow. When I take a long time to do something I'm thorough and deliberate.

When the other fellow doesn't do it, he's lazy. When I don't do it, I'm busy.

When the other fellow does it without being told, he's over-stepping his bounds. When I go ahead and do it without being told, that's initiative.

When the other fellow doesn't like my friends, he's prejudiced; when I don't like his, I'm simply showing good judgment of human nature.

When the other fellow states his opinion strongly, he's obstinate. When I state my opinion strongly, I'm firm.

When the other fellow picks flaws, he's cranky; when I do, I'm discriminating.

You cannot depend on your
evaluation of a person
when your imagination is
out of focus.

Procrastination

He had a year to do it in!
So he brushed the thought away;
A chap with half his energy
Might do it in a day.
A year! 'Twas too ridiculous,
As everyone should find;
However, he would get it done
And have it off his mind.

But not to-day. A few months hence
Would suit him better still;
Meanwhile, a far less irksome job
Might occupy his skill.
He would not let the matter pass
Entirely from him. No;

And doubtless he might take it up
In, say, a month or so.

He had six months to do it in!
For six long months had flown;
Well, why should that alarm a chap
With vigour like his own?
The job, when once embarked upon,
Would soon be rattled through;
However, he would think of it,
In, say, a week or two.

He had three months to do it in!
'Oh, brother!' was his cry:
'The thing hangs on me like a weight,
Each day that passes by.

Let's see: three months? Ah, that's enough;
But just to clear the doubt,
I'll make arrangements for a start
Before the month is out.'

He had a week to do it in!
And care was in his glance;
'It's hard,' he cried, 'that flight of time
Won't give a chap a chance.'
He still delayed; the swift week passed,
As weeks will ever run,
And though a year was given him,
The task was still undone.

"Never put off until tomorrow what you can do today," a wise man once said, "because if you enjoy it today, you can do it again tomorrow."

He slept beneath the moon,
He basked beneath the sun;
He lived a life of going-to-be,
And died with nothing done.

*Procrastination is the grave in
which opportunity is buried.*

Disorderliness

The police phoned a professor late at night to inform him that his office at the university had been vandalised. He was asked to go and verify if anything was missing. On his arrival he looked around the room in astonishment. Books and papers were scattered everywhere. His filing cabinet was open and several files were on the floor. The contents of a drawer had been spilt on the desk, the waste-paper-basket had been turned upside down, and a chair had been knocked over.

The professor was speechless as a police officer pointed out the broken window at the end of the corridor and explained that no other office along the corridor had been touched.

Finally the professor managed to speak. "But it's just as I left it!"

Borrowing

First one: "Good evening. Thought I'd drop in and see you about the book you borrowed from me last week."

Second one: "I'm sorry. But I lent it to a friend of mine. Did you want it?"

First one: "Well, not for myself, but the fellow I borrowed it from says the owner wants it."

A good neighbour is one who
doesn't expect you to return
the things you borrow.

Discouragement

Satan once decided to close shop, and put his tools on display for anyone who wished to buy them. Most prospective customers could identify Malice, Jealousy, and Pride. But one peculiar tool, which was by all appearances well used in its time, had the highest price-tag.

"What is that?" asked a curious customer.

"That is a very valuable tool," explained the devil. "It's called Discouragement. With it I could effectively break open people's hearts, without their realising what I was doing to them."

Aggression

In a *Peanuts* comic strip by Charles Schulz, the panels express aggression as a release of pent-up tension, as Linus manifests it: "I was trying to talk with that little girl up the street... but I couldn't say a word... I stood all embarrassed and confused. I got so self-conscious that I didn't know what to do... so I *hit* her."

Once upon a time there was a dog who was sitting by the side of the railway line when an express train roared by and cut off an inch of his tail. Seeking revenge, the dog waited patiently for the train's next trip, and tried to bite it as it went past. The train wheels ran right over the poor dog's neck, slicing off its head.

The moral of this little story is simple: Never lose your head over a little piece of tail.

Evil tendencies

A scorpion being a very poor swimmer, asked a turtle to carry him on his back across the river. "You must be out of your mind," said the turtle. "How can I do that? You'll sting me while I'm swimming and I'll drown."

"My dear turtle," laughed the scorpion, "if I were to sting you, you would drown and I would go down with you. Now, where is the logic in that?"

The turtle agreed, asked the scorpion to get on its back, and crawled into the river. Halfway across the deep waters, the scorpion gave the turtle a mighty sting, and they both began to sink. Resignedly, the turtle asked the scorpion, "Where's the logic now? Why did you do it?"

"My stinging has nothing to do with logic," the drowning scorpion sadly replied, "It's just my character."

An honest man asked his rich brother how he came into so much wealth while he remained poor.

"Because I have no scruples against doing wrong," came the answer.

So the man changed his ways. But in spite of all his cheating and corruption, he did not succeed in getting rich.

When he approached his brother again, he received this explanation: "The reason your wrongdoings have not made you wealthy is that you did them not from conviction that it matters not whether we do good or evil, but solely because you desired riches."

✳   ✳   ✳

TRAGICOMIC CHARACTERS

**Life is like a mirror.
If we frown at it, it frowns back.
If we smile, it returns the greeting.**

A. THE KILLJOYS

The Italian dramatist Luigi Pirandello, best known for his *Absurd* plays, tells the story of a man who was so frightened by joy that it drove him crazy.

After a long search he found the woman of his dreams; but he was so certain that he would lose her that he feigned disinterest until he almost did.

After he married her he planned a wonderful honeymoon. He told all his friends that they were going to Florence and Venice. But he actually took his bride to Naples — in the opposite direction.

It was his method of tricking Misery, which would be looking for him in the other places!

A person once asked his friend: "Why are you so glum-faced?"

"Well," he confided, "my wife insisted that I stop gambling, smoking, drinking and playing cards. So I did."

"I understand," said the other consolingly. "But at least your wife must be very happy."

"That's the problem. I thought she would be," cried his friend. "But now she acts so indifferent towards me — because she has nothing to complain about."

People whose main concern
is their own happiness,
seldom find it.

Yesterday I killed my son's joy
        In the victory of his team:
I complained about his dirty clothes
        And that ripped open seam.

Day before, I killed my daughter's pride
        In the dress that she had made:
I pointed out its faulty side,
        Then added my faint praise.

One day I killed a friendship
        And affection turned to hate;
I had misunderstood her mind,
        Until it was too late.

Today I killed my husband's love
        Not with a mighty blow;
It had died, bit by bit,
        Year by year — so slow:

I wounded him with cruel jibes
        When others too might hear
And when I saw him wince with pain
        Thought it unmanly fear.

Tonight I saw the light of love
        Die slowly in his look,
When he reached toward me his hand
        But I picked up the book.

> *Instead of letting their light*
> *shine, some people spend*
> *their time trying to put*
> *out the lights of others.*

A man who had a troubled marriage was pleasantly surprised when he returned home from work on his birthday and was presented with two neck-ties by his wife. He was overjoyed and decided to take her out to dinner. As he got dressed he wondered which of the ties to wear, for both were elegant-looking. He finally chose one.

As he turned to his wife, she stared at his neck and said in disgust, "So you didn't like the other one!"

In his book *The Right Distance*, Samuel F. Pickering makes a point about how our possessions weigh life down. He talks about the big yard that he possesses in front of his house. His friends tell him how fortunate he is to have it for his children to play in. But for him things are different.

His grass is not so green as he wants it, so he digs up his lawn and puts in some fertilisers. But he soon finds that a lot of weeds have cropped up, so he buys some weed-killers and sets about the operation of destroying the weeds. Once the weeds are cleared, he harrows up the yard, rakes it, scatters grass seed, and covers everything with straw. Then he spends days watering it....

During the whole process, of course, the children are not allowed to play on the lawn.

The tragedy of life is not that it ends so soon, but that we wait so long to begin it.

B. THE GULLIBLE

There was a notice outside which said: 'Cats for Sale'. The man entered the little Japanese house and noticed a kitten drinking milk from a bowl on the floor. But with his trained eye he saw at once that the bowl was priceless — a most unique piece of porcelain. He said to the owner, "I'll buy that cat. Will you take a 100 yen?" The owner agreed.

Then the customer asked, "By the way, the kitten might like to continue to drink from its own bowl so I'll take the bowl too. I'll give you 200 yen for the lot."

"Oh, no," said the owner, "that bowl is priceless."

"But why," asked the customer, "are you allowing a cat to drink from it on the floor?"

The man replied with a smile, "That's the way I sell cats."

A sign outside a bakery read: "Delicious Snaks."

Noticing the error, a person went in, bought some pastries, then tactfully asked the manager, "Didn't anyone tell you that your sign outside the shop is misspelled?"

"Oh, yes, many have," replied the man. "But then, it's good for business. The people who come in to tell me about it usually buy something before they leave."

❉   ❉   ❉

C. THE GARRULOUS

A neighbour asked a five-year-old boy, "Has your little sister learnt to talk yet?"

"Yes," replied the boy. "Now we are teaching her to be quiet."

The parents brought their son to a retired and highly respected teacher who conducted private classes for students in speech and debate.

The teacher interviewed the boy and found him to be an incorrigible chatterbox. She turned to the parents and said that she would take classes for the boy but she would charge twice the amount she normally did.

"Why so?" asked the young boy's father. "He is already quite fluent in his speech."

"Because," replied the teacher, "I must teach him two things instead of one — first, how to hold his tongue, and then how to use it."

"Father, did Edison make the first talking machine?"

"No, my son, God made the first talking machine, but Edison made the first one that could be cut off."

❊   ❊   ❊

A famous lecturer was asked the formula of success in public speaking.

"Well," he said, "in promulgating your esoteric cogitations and articulating superficial, sentimental and psychological observations, beware of platitudinous ponderosity. Let your extemporaneous decantations and unpremeditated expatiations have intelligibility and veracious veracity without rodomontade and thrasonical bombast. Sedulously avoid all polysyllabic profundity, pusillanimous vacuity, pestiferous profanity and similar transgressions.

"Or to put it a bit differently," he concluded smiling, "talk simply, naturally, and above all, don't use big words."

A man at the public booth seemed stuck to the telephone; though he looked bored, he made no attempt to speak. There was a crowd waiting outside. Getting impatient, the next in line opened the door and asked abruptly, "Are you speaking to anybody?"

The silent man replied, "Yes, to my wife."

Some people have eyes that see
not and ears that hear not, but
there are very few people who
have tongues that talk not.

D. THE 'DOWN-TO-EARTHERS'

A British newspaper once sponsored a contest for the best answer to this dilemma:

Three famous men — a nuclear physicist, a surgeon, and a computer engineer — who have made valuable contributions to humanity are travelling in a balloon. A severe storm arises, and to save the balloon, one of the passengers has to be thrown overboard. Which man should be sacrificed?

The paper received thousands of replies. Some competitors described at length the merits of each of the professionals.

But the judges awarded the first prize to a twelve-year-old whose answer was: "The fattest one."

A farmer was being interviewed by some sociology students. "Are your neighbours honest?" asked one student.

"They certainly are," replied the farmer.

"But I noticed a loaded gun in your sitting room," said the student. "How do you explain that?"

"That," answered the farmer, "is to keep them honest."

> *"You don't seem to realise on which*
> *side your bread is buttered."*
> *"What does it matter? I eat both sides."*

A man met his tailor a few days after he had collected his suit, and asked, "Why don't you send me a bill?"

The tailor explained that he never asked a gentleman for money.

The man asked what happened if someone did not pay.

"Oh," said the tailor, "after a certain time I conclude he is not a gentleman and then I ask him."

An elderly man was strolling on the beach when he came upon a magic lamp. As he picked it up, a genie suddenly appeared and said since he had found him, he would grant him a wish.

The aged gentleman thought for a while and then said, "My brother and I have not been on speaking terms for the past 25 years, after we had had a quarrel. I wish that my brother finally forgive me."

There was a thunderclap and the genie declared that the wish had been granted. But out of curiosity, the genie said: "Most people I appear to ask for wealth and fame. You, on the contrary, have asked for reconciliation and love. Is it because you are old and near death?"

"Not at all," cried the man. "But my brother is, and he's worth about 70 lakhs of rupees."

❈   ❈   ❈

E. THE DAREDEVILS

In July 1997, a 39-year-old Malaysian snake-charmer spent 21 days in a glass cage with a brood of temperamental room-mates — 6,000 scorpions. Ali Khan Samsuddin, who set a world record, was greeted with thunderous applause as he picked the last of the scorpions clinging to his body and stepped out of the cage. He looked hale and hearty despite the 99 stings he received.

Monitors kept watch to ensure Ali never left the three-metre by two-metre glass cage, in which plants and pieces of dead wood were strewn around to make the scorpions feel more at home. Ali slept on a mattress as scorpions scrambled over him.

Ali, dubbed the Scorpion King, has also set the world record for living together with poisonous snakes: he stayed with 400 cobras for 40 days daily from 10 a.m. to 10 p.m.

At 19, Pal Maharaja fell off a speeding train and lost his right leg. At 46, he had successfully scaled the M-Ten peak in the Himalayas, claiming to be the country's first handicapped mountaineer. All he does is fit a crude attachment to the tips of his indigenous crutches, and he is ready for the steepest climbs. Pal says he has never used oxygen for his incredible mountaineering feats. He sleeps in the open, in a plastic sheet, with two blankets. The only other possession he takes along is a cooking utensil.

Courage is not the absence
of fear but the conquest of it.

F. THE 'PLAYSAFERS'

Two state electricity board men were working on a set of wires. From the wall, two wires projected, one red and one blue. "Grab one of those wires, will you?" said one of the linesmen.

His friend said, "Sure," and took hold of the wire.

"Feel anything?"

"No."

"Good," said the first one. "I wasn't sure which was which. Now for God's sake don't touch the other one, or you'll drop dead."

The municipality was laying a drain line along the college wall. They came across a power cable lying directly in their path. The supervisor suspected that it was only an abandoned line, but, to be safe, called the college electrician to inspect it. The electrician arrived, looked at the cable, and assured the supervisor that it was dead. "Just cut it out of your way," he said.

"Are you sure there's no danger?" asked the supervisor.

"Absolutely," replied the electrician.

"Well, then, will you cut it for us?" requested the supervisor.

The electrician hesitated a moment, and with a slight smile said, "I'm not that sure."

❄️　　　❄️　　　❄️

G. THE STRATEGISTS

An Arabian Sheikh needed one more horse for his entourage before setting off on a trip into the desert. Two horses from a village nearby were brought to him, but the owner of each horse, not wanting to give up his animal, insisted his horse was worthless, broken-winded, crippled, old, and so on.

"It's a simple thing to settle," said the Sheikh. "We'll stage a race between the horses. The winning horse will be taken."

An adviser stepped forward: "It won't work, Your Highness. Neither man will let his horse ride fast."

"They will," said the Sheikh. "Let each man ride the other's horse!"

The second-graders were asked to raise money for an outreach programme the school was preparing. One little girl went to her neighbour's and explained her cause. To tease the girl, her neighbour placed a ten-rupee note and a 50-paisa coin on the table and told her to choose what she wished. The girl picked up the coin and said, "My mother always taught me to take the smaller piece."

Then picking up the note also, she added, "But so I won't lose this coin, I'll wrap it up in this piece of paper."

❄   ❄   ❄

A beggar in a town market was considered to be a silly fellow, so people used to amuse themselves by making him choose between a one rupee coin and a 50 paisa coin. He always chose the latter, even when persuaded to take the larger amount.

One day another beggar tried to make him understand how he was being made a laughing stock, and must stop that by taking the larger coin.

The first beggar said: "I prefer behaving like a fool. Don't you realise how much people `pay' me for being amused? If I start acting smart they will not be interested in me any more."

Two friends were returning home late at night after their card games.

One said: "I'm always afraid to go home after late-night parties. I switch off the engine of my car well before I reach the house and coast into the garage. I take off my shoes and sneak into the house. I try to be as quiet as possible, but invariably, as I slip into bed, my wife sits up and starts berating me."

The other man said: "You just have the wrong strategy. I never have any trouble. I keep the car-engine running even as I enter the garage. I slam the front door and stomp into the house, creating quite a racket. Then I go to the bedroom, pat my wife, and say, `How're things?' She always pretends she is asleep."

❈   ❈   ❈

Outside a supermarket, two boys saw an old woman drop her purse on the street and walk away. One of the boys quietly ran and grabbed it. Since they knew where the woman lived, the other insisted that they return it.

The boy agreed on one condition. "There are only big notes in it," he said, "let us change one of them to smaller ones." He wanted to make sure of the tip!

One day a man went fishing but had hard luck. Not wanting to go home empty-handed, he went to a shop to buy some fish. He told the dealer: "Just stand where you are, and throw me five of the biggest fish you have."

"But why throw them?" asked the dealer in amazement.

"So I can tell my family I caught them," replied the man. "I may be a poor fisherman, but I'm no liar."

A man walking down his street was confronted by a stranger who asked him if he knew where to find the new restaurant. The man said he did, and proceeded to give detailed directions. The stranger thanked him and started off in the wrong direction. The man shouted, "The restaurant is the other way."

"Oh, I know that," replied the stranger. "I'm the new owner, and I'm making sure everybody knows where it is."

❄   ❄   ❄

In a large bungalow lived a rich old woman, who possessed a valuable antique vase. The vase had a peculiar but enticing colour. One day it got into her head to have her living room painted the same colour as the vase. She offered to pay a handsome amount to the painter who could produce a shade which perfectly matched that of the vase.

Several painters tried their hand but failed to produce the exact shade. One of them, however, returned some days later, and assured her that he had found the right colour paint. She left him to prepare a sample on a square sheet of canvas.

When she came in to inspect the result a little later, she saw that the colour on the canvas matched that of the vase perfectly. She was so pleased that she asked him to paint not only the living room, but the entire house as well. She spoke so appreciatively of his skills to her friends, that the painter was soon highly in demand and eventually became rich and famous.

Years later, when the painter's son took over the business, he said to the father: "Dad, how did you manage to get the exact shade of colour on the canvas as that of the vase?"

"It was simple," replied the father. "I painted the vase."

❋   ❋   ❋

H. THE LEGALISTS

At an army headquarters, a Duty Officer summoned the Regimental Sergeant Major (RSM) and asked him to find out how high the guard-room flagpole was. The RSM went to the guard-room and ordered the sentry to take one end of the measuring tape he held out, climb the pole, and hold the tape-end at the top.

The sentry suggested that it would be simpler to take the pins out of the bottom of the pole, lay it to the ground, and then measure it.

The RSM snapped: "The officer wants to know how high it is, not how long it is, so get up that pole."

In a federal building in the U.S. an employee wanted to get rid of a big stack of out-dated documents and reports. He heaped them on top of his waste basket with a large sign reading: "Rubbish."

The following day he found the papers still there so he added the words *Please Remove* to his note. The next day he discovered that the stack had not been touched, so he scrawled a fresh notice using a red-tipped marker for effect: *THIS IS RUBBISH. I DO NOT WANT IT. PLEASE REMOVE IT.*

On the fourth day the stack remained intact, but below his sign was a small note in pencil: *Cannot remove unless marked 'Trash'.*

❋   ❋   ❋

A passenger on a luxury bus asked the conductor, "Is smoking permitted, mister?"

"No."

"Well, where did all these cigarette butts and all this smoke come from?"

The man in uniform replied: "From people who didn't ask questions."

The bus passenger with a pipe in his mouth was sitting under the 'No Smoking' sign. When the conductor pointed out the sign, the passenger replied, "I'm not smoking."

"But you've got a pipe in your mouth," protested the conductor.

"So what," the passenger retorted. "I have my shoes on, but I'm not walking."

A widow was selling her husband's brand new Maruti car for Rs 500 only. When someone asked her why she was throwing away such an expensive car, the widow explained: "In my husband's will, he asked that his new Maruti be sold and the proceeds be given to his beautiful young secretary. I'm following his wishes — to the letter."

❄   ❄   ❄

I. THE OUTWITTERS

The fussy old millionaire was interviewing a man. "I want a very careful chauffeur," he said. "I want a man who takes no risks at all."

"I'm just the man for you," said the applicant. "Can I have my salary in advance?"

A baker was so stingy that he was upset with the poor man who begged for alms near his shop. The baker felt that anyone who even smelled his delicious products should pay for the privilege. So he took the beggar to court.

The judge listened patiently to the accuser, then asked the beggar if he had any money. The poor man produced a handful of small coins. The judge took them. The judge jingled the coins together and returned them to the beggar. Then he addressed the court: "The punishment should match the crime. The price for the smell of bread shall be the sound of money."

A worker received Rs 5 less in his pay envelope, and complained to the paymaster. "You were overpaid Rs 5 last week and didn't object," reasoned the paymaster.

"I know," said the employee. "I don't mind overlooking one mistake, but when it happens the second time, I think it's time to complain."

❈   ❈   ❈

A woman was driving her car at about 80 miles an hour, when she noticed a motor-cycle cop following her. She didn't slow down; she figured, maybe, she could shake him off by doing 90. When she looked back again, there were two motor cycles following her. She boosted her speed again. The next time she looked, three motor cycles were screaming along behind her.

Suddenly she saw a service station looming ahead. She screeched to a stop in front of it, dashed out and ran into the Ladies Toilet.

Ten minutes later, she walked demurely out. The three cops were standing right there, waiting for her. Without batting an eyelid, she said coyly, "I'll bet you thought I wouldn't make it."

A few months after their marriage, the wife, clearly upset with her husband squeezing the toothpaste in the middle, in spite of her telling him often not to, decided to stick a note on the tube which said: "Please squeeze me at the bottom."

The husband made no comments about it, but much to her satisfaction, started to obey the instruction.

Months later, the woman decided to make one of her very rare cakes. Taking the pan out of the cupboard she noticed a note attached to it: "Please use me more often."

The longest odds in the world
are those against getting even
with someone.

J. THE ECCENTRICS

At a restaurant, one evening, a woman called the waiter and requested that the air-conditioner be turned down. A few minutes later, the lady was fanning herself, and she signalled for the waiter. This time she asked him to turn up the air-conditioning. Some time later she had it turned down, and up again.

A man seated at the next table, who had been keenly observing the proceedings, sympathised with the waiter. "She must be driving you crazy," he noted.

"Not in the least," replied the waiter, "I'm driving *her* crazy. We don't have any air-conditioning."

The members of a church choir had several rehearsals in preparation for the Christmas Midnight service. At every session there would be members missing, except one who was very regular.

At the final rehearsal, the choirmaster called for attention and said, "I wish to offer a special vote of thanks to Alfred, our second lead singer, for being the only one to attend every rehearsal."

"I thought I should do at least that much," commented Alfred, "since I won't be present for the Midnight service."

Nobody don't never get nothing for
nothing nowhere, no time, nohow.

The manager for long suspected that a particular worker was stealing from the factory. So whenever this guy left the factory, he was thoroughly frisked. But everytime, they found that he carried nothing in his clothes and his wheelbarrow was empty.

Finally, when the worker retired, the manager couldn't resist asking how he had stashed a fortune beyond his means. "Simple," came the reply. "I stole wheelbarrows."

A man wore shoes that were so tight-fitting that he limped and his feet became sore. When asked why he did it, he said that his business had failed, his wife had divorced him, and his son was misbehaving.

"But what has that got to do with your shoes?" someone asked.

"Fact is," explained the man, "I feel miserable all day. The only time I feel good is when I go home and take off my shoes."

A miser once took his wife to a picnic. Looking at an ice-cream stall he asked: "Will you have another ice-cream cone?"

"Another cone?" she exclaimed, "What do you mean by another cone? Where is the first?"

"Oh..." the miser said, "Have you forgotten I bought you a cone last year?"

❄   ❄   ❄

A man at a friend's house sat brooding over a cup of tea. He said, "I tell you, Sam, I don't know what I'm going to do about my wife."

"What is it now?" asked his friend.

"The same old thing — money. She is always asking for money. Only last Monday she wanted thirty rupees; yesterday she was around asking for fifty, and this morning, if you please, she demanded eighty rupees."

"What does she do with all the money, for heaven's sake?" asked the friend.

"There is no way of finding out. I never give her any."

Pundit Bholabhai owned an apple orchard that was the pride of the town. So, naturally, it attracted the neighbourhood kids who would sneak in to steal the fruit. The Pundit would keep constant vigil. He would allow the children to pluck the apples, then dash out with shotgun in hand, threatening to shoot them if they came again. This went on for several weeks.

A curious neighbour asked Bholabhai: "What's wrong with you, Pundit? You've a dozen times more apples in your orchard than you can probably use for the family. Why don't you allow the kids to take some?"

"Well, well," replied Bholabhai with a laugh, "of course I want them to have the apples. I know how it was when I was a boy. If I don't create a scene and chase them, these kids will never come back!"

The greatest lesson in life
is to realise that even
fools are right sometimes.

K. THE SELFISH

There is a parable about a man in hell who prayed so fervently to be released from his torments the Lord granted his wish. A voice told him to go to the brink of hell from where he would be rescued. When he reached the place, a carrot held by a slender thread was let down and he was asked to grasp it.

As he held onto the thin string he was surprised that it could bear his weight. Slowly he felt himself being lifted up. However, the other inmates realised what was happening and they rushed to the spot and seized the man's fireproof garments, in the hope that they too might be rescued with him.

The man, however, was irked by the idea that others were taking advantage of his prayer, and he began to kick them off, saying that the thread would break. And, indeed, it did break.

But a voice was heard from above: The thread was strong enough to save both you and your brothers and sisters; but it was not strong enough to save you alone.

It has been found that English is the only major language in which "I" is capitalised. In many other languages, "You" is capitalised and the "i" is in lower case.

When two egotists meet it's
a case of an"I" for an "I".

L. THE IRRESPONSIBLE

The following are cuttings from recent newspapers about reports of people who have been negligent, irresponsible in executing their duties to the extent of causing the death of innocents.

June 13, 1997: At least 60 people were killed and around 200 injured when a major fire broke out at the multi-storeyed Uphaar cinema hall in South Delhi. About 1,000 cinegoers who were present in the hall were jolted by an explosion that took place in the basement of the building at around 5 p.m. The lights went off, and smoke oozed in through the air-conditioning ducts. Most people died of asphyxiation.

A short circuit in the transformer led to 500 litres of transformer oil catching fire. The situation was aggravated because once the transformer collapsed, the staff switched on the generators thinking it to be a case of routine power failure. With the generators on, the blowers of the AC plant kept working. This resulted in the smoke spreading quickly and the balcony was engulfed with toxic air.

The manager of the theatre knew the transformer was defective, but did not replace it in spite of earlier mishaps. The hall was not equipped with smoke alarms, or emergency exits, or fire-safety technology.

Concluded an editorial: "Such tragedies only underline our own callousness as a people towards fire and electric safety, our lack of civic sense, or simply our fatalistic outlook towards life."

❄   ❄   ❄

July 4, 1997: In the worst-ever tragedy, at least 33 people met their watery grave when a private luxury bus they were travelling in was swept away in the swirling waters of the Bhogavo river, 40 km from Dhandhuka town in Gujarat. Only seventeen passengers had a miraculous escape.

The bus had started behind schedule. Since the driver was speeding up, he was advised to go slow. At two places the bus narrowly escaped from meeting accidents. After this, a sense of fear gripped the passengers. At a stopover in Dhandhuka, the driver was missing for nearly an hour-and-a-half, adding to the tension. When he came, passengers found him in a bad shape of mind, perhaps drunk.

"From Dhandhuka onwards it was simply a reckless driving, leaving everybody tense," said survivors. Some passengers even warned the driver. However, their plea went unheeded.

When the bus entered Loliya village, they told him that he should drive carefully as the Bhogavo river was in spate. When the bus neared a bridge, the driver ignored the barricades put up by the local villagers to prevent traffic using the ground-level parallel road across the river-bed, instead of the bridge.

The passengers soon found the bus surrounded by the flowing waters, but the driver said he could not see the flood waters.... Then the bus began to sink; the strong current of the river broke the window panes; water entered the bus. The bus tumbled. Those passengers who managed to break open the door and get out were swept away in the force of the river.

> *The hand that lifts the cup*
> *that "cheers" should not be*
> *used to shift the gears.*

July 22, 1997: Ten children were killed and 40 injured, six of them seriously, when the roof of a *madrasa* on the outskirts of Meerut city collapsed at 1.30 a.m. on Tuesday after heavy rains.

The *madrasa* was built in August last year in 10 days. So fragile was the building that it could not take the weight of even the thick mud plaster that passed for a roof.

The District Magistrate said: "Action will be taken against the civic officials who allowed this building to come up without permission."

July 29, 1997: At 11 p.m. on Sunday, the KK Express collided with the Himsagar Express at Old Faridabad Railway Station, leaving 12 people dead and 82 injured. The accident occurred when the driver of KK Express, overlooking three red signals, one after another, hit the rear end of the stationary Himsagar Express. While the general bogey of the Himsagar was smashed, the AC sleeper car got locked between the two trains. This indicates that the driver and the assistant of the KK Express were either sleeping or trying to make up for lost time. The train was running eight hours behind schedule.

Elaborating on the details of the general procedure, the Superintendent of Police said, "The assistant driver repeatedly indicates the signals to the driver and in return, the driver pronounces the signal's position to him to avoid any confusion. Overlooking three consecutive signals clearly suggests that the driver and his assistant neglected their duty."

❋   ❋   ❋

Recently there has been renewed interest in the 'Titanic', with the making of the most expensive movie. When the world's largest ocean liner steamed majestically through the darkness on her maiden voyage to New York on 14th April 1912, there were more than two thousand people enjoying the liner's snug comfort. It struck an iceberg in the Atlantic near Nova Scotia, then sank, killing 1,500 passengers. The cause of the tragedy is recorded by the *Washington Post*:

In the wheelroom, a nattily uniformed officer hummed at his task as he directed the destinies of an ocean greyhound that even then was setting a speed record.

The phone rang. A minute passed! Another minute! The officer, his trivial task completed, stepped to the phone. From the 'crow's nest' — "Iceberg dead ahead! Reverse engines!" But too late. As he rushed to the controls, the 'pride of the seas' crashed into the iceberg amid a deafening roar.

Three precious minutes! Attention to trivial details and sixteen hundred people paid with their lives.

Playwright Moss Hart once confessed: "All the mistakes I ever made in my life were when I wanted to say `No,' and said `Yes.'"

> *None of us is responsible for all the things that happen to us, but we are responsible for the way we act when they do happen.*

M. THE CHEATS

A contractor for a construction company used to routinely cheat on materials that went into the houses that he built. But he made the exteriors look so attractive that none of the owners suspected he had used inferior materials.

Before his retirement he was given his final construction project. It was to be a luxury home. Since this was his last opportunity to make money, he cheated on it gloriously, using as much inferior material as possible, and inflating all the bills.

When the house was completed the manager of the company came to inspect it. It looked fantastic. He congratulated the contractor. Then he called the construction workers together and said he had a very special announcement to make.

"Our contractor is about to retire. As a mark of gratitude for his many years of service," he said, turning to the contractor, "the company has decided to gift him with this luxury house which he himself has constructed!" The contractor almost collapsed!

A woman used to get very upset with the milkman, who consistently watered down the milk. One day she said to him in a seemingly sympathetic tone: "It must be very tiring for you, climbing all those stairs in the heat with those heavy buckets. Why don't you just bring the milk, and we'll add the water up here?"

❄   ❄   ❄

A woman goes to the electricity company to pay her bill. She gets twenty rupees too much in change. But she decides to keep it. She rationalises thus: The company has more money than I've got. They are all big crooks anyway. They must have cheated me many times. I'll keep this just to get even.

"One cannot be careful enough these days," said the daughter to her mother on her return from work. "There are too many cheats around the place. This morning, when I handed over a 50-rupee note to the clerk towards the office tea-club, he at once pointed out that the bill was a fake."

"That's too bad," said her mother. "Let me have a look at it."

"Oh, I don't have it," said the young girl cheerfully, "I managed to get rid of it. The unsuspecting man at the snack-bar took it."

Three college students were at a loose end.

"What'll we do tonight?" asked one.

"I've an idea," said another. "Let's toss a coin. It it's heads, we'll go to the cafeteria. It it's tails, we'll go to the movies. And if it stands on edge, we'll study!"

❋   ❋   ❋

A baker and a farmer made a contract. The baker would send a pound of bread to the farmer in exchange for a pound of butter. Things worked out fine for quite a while. Then one day the baker became suspicious that the butter weighed less. For several days he kept a check and found the weight of the butter decreasing. Finally he had the farmer arrested for fraud.

At the trial the judge was surprised when the farmer told him he had scales but no weights. How did he weigh the butter, then, inquired the judge.

"It is like this," the farmer explained, "I take the one-pound bread and place in on the scale to weigh the butter."

The baker was caught at his own game and had to pay a fine to the farmer.

Looking for an inexpensive gift, a stingy lady entered a shop, but found everything too expensive. Finally, she found a glass vase that had been broken and costing almost nothing. She asked the shopkeeper to send it, hoping her friend would think it had been broken in transit.

In due time she received an acknowledgement. "Thanks for the vase," it read, "and it was so thoughtful of you to wrap each piece separately."

❄ ❄ ❄

One of the inmates of the lunatic asylum was watching another play patience. "Just one moment," said the first suddenly, "I've just caught you cheating yourself."

The other put his finger to his lips and looked around. "Shh!" he whispered. "Don't tell anyone, but I've been cheating myself for years."

"You don't mean it?" replied the first lunatic.

"Don't you ever catch yourself cheating?"

"No," said the player, shaking his head. "I'm too clever."

There is an Indian folk tale of a king who decided to offer a grand banquet to the residents of one of the villages in his kingdom. He asked the villages for a small contribution. Each of them, he said should bring only one jug of milk on the morning of the celebration, and deposit it in a huge vessel that would be provided.

When the day arrived, one villager thought, "I will go with my jug when it is still dark, filling it with water instead of milk; after all, a jug of water in such a large vessel of milk will hardly make a difference."

When the king's cooks came to collect the vessel of milk, all they found in it was water. Every villager thought that if he cheated by bringing a bowl of water, no one would notice it!

❋   ❋   ❋

One morning a recently married couple received two theatre tickets with a note which read: "Guess who sent these."

On the appointed evening they went to the theatre, still wondering who could have sent them the tickets for such a good show. When they reached home rather late, they were shocked to find that all their wedding presents had been stolen.

On the table of their drawing room they found a note in the same writing as the previous one, saying: "Now you know."

A boy had been brought into court again, charged with stealing jewellery. The magistrate determined to appeal to his father.

"See here," said the judge, "this boy of yours has been in court many times charged with theft, and I am tired of seeing him here."

"I don't blame you, Judge," said the father. "And I am just as tired of seeing him here as you are."

"Then why don't you teach him how to act? Show him the right way and he will not be coming here."

"I have already shown him the right way," said the father, "but he just does not seem to have any talent for learning. He always gets caught."

❋ ❋ ❋

N. THE EXPLOITERS

Mastan, an 18-year-old boy from Bangalore, ran away from home with a meagre Rs 250, and travelled to Mumbai. Illiterate and penniless, Mastan could not find a job for himself. However, the youth came to know of the Haji Ali dargah (Muslim saint's tomb) where food is distributed free. For about 40 days he ate at the dargah during the day and slept on the pavement at night. He then fell sick with high temperature and cough. In what seemed like a God-send help, a man approached him and offered to take him to a hospital in a taxi. Mastan accompanied him and through lanes and by-lanes they drove for about a quarter of an hour and reached a 'hospital'. After being kept under treatment for nearly ten days, occasionally visited by a doctor, Mastan was finally freed.

"They gave me Rs 5,000 and asked me to go back to my home town," he said. A man escorted him to the railway station, apparently because he could not walk on his own. The whole incident was a bit too much for the credulous boy to take and he bribed his escort Rs 2,000 only to be told that his kidney had been taken out.

A factory worker refused to join a group scheme. No policy could be issued until all employees signed, but he held out stubbornly. The foreman begged him to sign; the shop steward pleaded with him; the factory manager asked him. Still no go. At last the owner of the factory took him aside and said, "Listen, you idiot. Unless you sign, I'll fire you." The worker grabbed the paper and signed immediately.

"Now," asked the owner, "why didn't you sign this thing before?"

"Because," the man replied, "no one explained it as clearly as you did, sir."

❄   ❄   ❄

A woman visited the house of a certain person called Sunita in the latter's village in north-west Bengal and told her family wonderful stories about Mumbai — the city of dreams. The poverty-stricken family was convinced that their daughter, abandoned by her husband for giving birth to a girl, stood a better chance of survival in Mumbai. They were so impressed by the woman's story that they allowed Sunita's ten-year-old sister also to accompany her.

The dream broke soon after they arrived in Mumbai. Sunita was forced into prostitution and when she tried to shield her younger sister, the manageress of the whorehouse demanded Rs 20,000 for the little one's freedom. Left with no choice, Sunita decided to pay the amount by working for the manageress. She was assured that her sister would be kept in safe custody till Sunita had put in Rs 20,000 worth of service. Then her sister would be set free.

Driven by poverty, a couple was forced to sell their seven-month-old daughter for Rs 1,000 to their neighbour in north Delhi's Indira Camp area.

The bizarre incident came to light when the child's mother, Munni Devi, 27, had a change of heart a few days after striking the deal. She and her husband tried to persuade the 'adopted parents' to give back the child, saying they had made a wrong decision and wanted to rectify the mistake. The latter, however, reportedly refused to return the child, claiming that they had the transaction in writing.

Finally, through police intervention, the child was returned to her mother.

❊   ❊   ❊

This is a bizarre and inhuman story. Three brothers, members of a family in Mailapur in Tamil Nadu, suffer from a syndrome known as Ananecephaly, which is a deformity that makes the head flat, eyes and tongue protrude. These physically deformed and mentally disabled brothers are made to travel all over the country where exhibitions are held.

They are locked in a cage and exhibited as "living examples of Darwin's theory" — according to the hoarding. A cassette playing continuously outside the stall proclaims: "Their every action is human but they are neither humans nor animals. They pose a challenge to anthropologists." The agent conducting the `live show' says the brothers are kept in prison round the clock. "We make sure they are under-fed, otherwise they go off to sleep immediately."

For Rs 3, visitors can take a look at these "half-humans playing with dogs and making monkey gestures." When the `show' is on, they are made to obey the `trainer's' orders — and ask for alms.

The diamond cutting and polishing industry at Bhavnagar in Gujarat, clandestinely employs a number of children in violation of the child-labour Act. The children are forced to work long hours, in poor conditions; as many as 15 to 20 of them are huddled together in a limited space surrounded by machines. No provision is made to protect their eyes. Their exposure to dust, and lack of ventilation, put them in danger of contracting tuberculosis and other lung-related diseases. They are under-paid and provided with no housing. After work they have to return to miserable houses which lack the basic necessities.

Complaints to the employers go unheeded. They, after all, are only interested in the business.

❈   ❈   ❈

A woman suffering from infertility made the headlines after she delivered septuplets — seven babies, in November 1997. Bobbi McCaughey was treated with the ovulation-stimulating drug called Metrodin.

Before the McCaughey babies, the most famous multiple births — by far — were the Dionne quintuplets, five identical girls naturally born to a French-Canadian farmer and his wife in Corbeil, Ontario, on May 28, 1934. The media got wind of the event when the father called the local newspaper to ask whether a birth announcement for five babies would cost the same as one.

An enterprising journalist filed a wire-service report, and the quints became global celebrities. Three Hollywood movies were made of their lives; in the midst of the Depression, sales of Dionne dolls outstripped those of Shirley Temple.

The Canadian government saw the five girls as a welcome tonic for a beleaguered Depression era public. By an act of Ontario's parliament, they were taken from their parents and exhibited three times a day behind glass at a facility christened Quintland.

At one point they drew more tourists than the Niagara Falls. Two of the girls died young — one of a seizure, one of a stroke; the others have survived but remain embittered and have petitioned for compensation for their mistreatment.

Recently, the three emerged from seclusion to offer advice to the McCaugheys, in an open letter, in which they said, "... We hope your children receive more respect than we did. Their fate should be no different from that of other children. Multiple births should not be confused with entertainment, nor should they be an opportunity to sell products."

❋   ❋   ❋

A struggling Iranian writer, working as a salesman at a bookstore, had published many of his short stories in literary magazines. But he was crazy about writing a 'realistic' novel.

In order to gather 'realistic' material for this work of fiction, which he hoped would be a best-seller, he would lock his wife up for hours and stare at her through a window above the door, taking notes of her reactions. At times he would strike her, on various pretexts, and then would scrutinise her and take notes as she was squirming in pain.

After the ordeal, he would stroke and comfort his wife, and ask her to forgive him. She has filed for divorce, but the man said he would not consent to it.

"I was only taking advantage of slight problems between us to write a book about bitter-sweet experiences of life," he said, in apparent vindication of his sadistic behaviour.

In September 1977, Mrs Ranjan Gandhi's body was fished out from the canal near Tarapur. Investigations revealed that Ranjan was tortured and mentally harassed by her husband, father-in-law, and brother-in-law. From the very next day of her marriage, they made dowry demands on her. In spite of her family threatening the in-laws with legal action, they kept on demanding a TV, Refrigerator and scooter. Ranjan's father then started sending cheques of Rs 500 every month. But the 'torture' continued unabated, till Ranjan took her life.

❀   ❀   ❀

O. THE MURDERERS

Three gangsters kidnapped a jeweller, murdered him, and took his jewel case to their hideout in the suburbs. There they planned to divide the jewels. Two went into the hideout at once, but the youngest gangster was sent to the town for a bottle of whisky.

While he was gone, one of the older men said, "Say, why should we give that kid a third of the jewels? When he comes back we'll give him the works and share fifty-fifty."

Meanwhile the younger man was thinking, "Those two will double-cross me if they can. Why shouldn't I have the whole jewel box myself and be a rich man? All that's needed is a little poison in the whisky I'm supposed to bring back."

So he bought some poison at a drugstore and put it into the whisky.

As soon as he got inside the cottage and put the bottle on the table, one of the gangsters shot him dead from behind; then they sat down and divided the jewels while they drank the poisoned whisky.

In an hour, they were both dead. The police found all three bodies, traced the shopkeepers who sold the whisky and the poison, and were able to find out what had happened.

Once we thought the world was
flat, then round. Now we know
a lot of it is crooked.

The following two items appeared one below the other in the newspapers on June 18, 1997. They reveal how cheaply some people value human life.

Rajendra Gurjar, the owner of a *pan-galla* (street-side stall selling edible leaves and condiments), had a quarrel with a cobbler, Chhaganbhai Chamar, over the issue of repairing a shoe, on Tuesday. After a heated exchange, Rajendra inflicted several blows on Chhaganbhai with a sharp weapon and injured him seriously.

Police who were patrolling the area found the cobbler lying in a pool of blood, with the culprit fleeing towards a residential area. They gave him hot chase and succeeded in nabbing him. Chhaganbhai died in hospital.

A youth, Mahendra Goswami, was sentenced to life imprisonment by the sessions judge, on a charge of murder. Last May, another youth, Girish Thakore, had made some comments about the sister of Mahendra, who took strong objection to it. Both had a heated exchange after which the enraged Mahendra inflicted knife blows on Girish, killing him on the spot.

❄   ❄   ❄

HUMAN
NATURE

Man is a piece of the
universe made alive.

R.W. Emerson

A. TWISTS IN THE TALE

Two friends met on a street one day. The first said:

"Well, Tom, I read in the papers this morning that your rich aunt passed away."

"That's right," said the other. "Just imagine, I spent the last eight years pretending I was fond of her darn cats so she would remember me in her will."

"Is that so? And what did she leave you?"

"The cats."

A man always left his bicycle in his courtyard at night after he got back from work. One morning he found his bicycle missing. He lamented the loss, but was not in a position to buy a new one immediately.

Three days later, however, to his pleasant surprise, he discovered his bicycle back in its place. Attached to the handlebars was a note:

"Sir, I had to borrow your bicycle, otherwise I would have missed a very important appointment. I regret the inconvenience caused you. As a mark of gratitude, I'm attaching a new lock to it. I'm sure it will be more effective than the old one."

*　　*　　*

At a crossroads, waiting for the traffic lights to change, an elderly lady stood beside another with a twin-baby carriage. The cute infants were fast asleep. The elderly lady got talking to the other, asking her how old the babies were, how much they weighed, whether they behaved well, and if they were girls or boys. The lady with the carriage pointing, said, "That's a boy, and that's a girl."

"Aren't you lucky," said the elderly lady.

"I certainly am," replied the other. "They belong to my sister."

A very old man with a weak heart won eighty thousand pounds in a football pool in England. His family, fearing that the good news might prove fatal for his fragile heart, called in the vicar to break it to him. "Now, John," began the vicar cautiously, "suppose you were to win one of these big prizes — eighty thousand pounds, say, — what would you do with it?"

The old man pondered. "Well, Father," he said, "to start with I'd give you half of it for the church." The vicar fell dead.

One priest told his congregation that there are 572 different sins mentioned in the Bible. He received numerous requests for the list from people who thought they might be missing something.

✳   ✳   ✳

A young author once told Mark Twain that he was losing confidence in his ability to write. "Did you ever get that feeling yourself?" he asked.

"Yes," said Twain. "Once, after I had been writing for nearly fifteen years, it suddenly struck me that I did not possess the slightest talent for writing."

"What did you do then? Did you give up writing?"

"How could I? By then I was already famous."

A young man was perturbed because he was too diffident to approach the opposite sex. He thought he should educate himself in this important matter. So he entered a bookshop, inspected the stacks, and spied, on a high shelf, what he thought would help him. It was a big volume called PERCEPTION to SEX.

He took it out quietly, and approached the cashier. He paid a huge amount for it, carried it home, and after his supper, settled himself in a comfortable chair to read it. Only then did he discover that what he had bought was part of an encyclopedia.

An authority on art was giving a lecture on famous paintings, painters and the history of the world of art. He talked on and on, covering the situation from ancient to modern times. When he finally finished his talk he asked, "Are there any questions?"

A little old lady in the rear of the hall raised her hand. "What kind of oil did you use on the floor to make it so shiny?"

*   *   *

There was a large lake in front of a mental hospital. One day a patient jumped over the fence into the lake and started to drown. Another patient ran in and pulled him out. The psychiatrist asked him why he did it.

"Why doctor, this crazy nut can't swim. If I hadn't gone in and pulled him out he'd have drowned!"

"I know, I know," said the psychiatrist, "but *what* made you do it?"

"But doctor, it was the thoughtful, kindly, brotherly thing to do!"

"I can't understand why you are a patient here," said the psychiatrist; "if you can tell me the same story tomorrow morning then I will personally discharge you."

The next morning he sent for the patient. "Now tell me in your own words, what happened yesterday."

"Doctor, what is there to tell? This crazy nut jumped into the lake and started to drown. I jumped after him and pulled him out, because if I hadn't he'd be a dead duck. It was the thoughtful, humane thing to do. I did it for him, I'd do it for you, I'd do it for anyone."

"That's enough," said the psychiatrist, "I'm impressed. You're discharged! Before you leave, I have something very sad to tell you. Right after you pulled that man out of the lake he hanged himself."

"No, doctor, he didn't hang himself," said the patient, "I did it! I just hung him up to dry him out!"

✳   ✳   ✳

Whenever Richard Cory went down town,
    We people on the pavement looked at him:
He was a gentleman from sole to crown,
    Clean favoured, and imperially slim.

And he was always quietly arrayed,
    And he was always human when he talked;
But still he fluttered pulses when he said,
    "Good-morning," and he glittered when he walked.

And he was rich — yes, richer than a king,
    And admirably schooled in every grace:
In fine, we thought that he was everything
    To make us wish that we were in his place.

So on we worked, and waited for the light,
    And went without the meat, and cursed the bread;
And Richard Cory, one calm summer night,
    Went home and put a bullet through his head.

A tired, starving hunter emerged from the forest where he had been wandering, dropped his rifle and ran to embrace a stranger who just entered the clearing from the opposite direction.

"Thank heaven, mister!" he exclaimed. "I've been lost for two days. Am I glad to see you!"

"What are you so glad about?" murmured the other man. "I've been lost for a week!"

*　　*　　*

B. PARADOXES

Photographer: "I've been taking wedding pictures for years."

Friend: "Tell me, who would you say smiles the most at a wedding — the bride or the groom?"

Photographer: "The bride's father."

A beggar stopped a man on the street and asked for some money for something to eat. The man said, "I'll buy you a drink if you like."

The beggar said, "I never drink."

"Well, then," said the man, "I'll buy you a good cigar."

"But I don't smoke," said the beggar. "All I want is something to eat."

"I've got a good tip for a horse this afternoon," said the man, "and I'll put some money on it for you. You can have the winnings."

"But I don't believe in gambling. All I want is food."

"In that case," said the man, "I'd like you to come home to dinner with me. I'd like my wife to meet you because I want her to know what happens to a man who doesn't smoke, drink or gamble."

✳   ✳   ✳

On one of his flights a pilot nudged his co-pilot and said: "See that beautiful lake down there and the village perched on the hill next to it. I was born there. As a child my hobby was to go fishing in the lake. Then I used to look at the planes flying overhead and dream of becoming a pilot. Today I wish I had time to go back to the village and do some fishing to relax."

The telephone at a rectory in New York rang at about 2 o'clock on a cold, blustering morning. "I think grandpa is dying," an excited voice declared to the priest. Since the address given was only a short distance away, the priest decided to walk.

As he passed an alley a figure with a gun stepped out and demanded, "Give me your money."

The priest told the gunman, "My purse is in the pocket of my coat."

He opened his coat to get it, revealing his Roman collar. "Oh, I didn't know you were a priest," stuttered the mugger. "Pardon me, Father. Keep your money."

In grateful relief Father offered him a cigarette but the fellow shook his head: "No thanks, Father, I'm not smoking during Lent."

> *Religion is not a way of looking*
> *at certain things. It is a certain*
> *way of looking at everything.*

When a burglar crept up to the safe in a large house, he found a note stuck to it: Please do not use explosives. This safe is not locked. Just turn the knob. The moment he turned the knob a sand-bag fell on him, the lights went on, and the alarm sounded. He was caught red-handed.

When a friend visited him in prison, he found him very bitter. "How am I ever going to trust any human being again?" moaned the thief.

A young man applied for a job as a bell-hop in a luxury hotel. His intelligent responses impressed the interviewers and he was accepted on probation.

He was a very active, pleasant and enterprising person, and was soon appreciated by everyone; but unfortunately, he was illiterate, and this became a serious handicap when he was sent on errands. So he lost the job.

Yet, the intelligent man was not let down. He travelled to Billimora, near Surat, and got a job polishing diamonds. And, to make a long story short, he eventually owned a thriving diamond business.

In the course of a newspaper interview, the reporter said, "I'm impressed by your success story. Just imagine what you would be if you could read and write."

"Oh," said the illiterate businessman, "I know what I would have been — a bell-hop in a hotel."

*   *   *

C. REVEALING CONCLUSIONS

"You stopped drinking, gambling and loafing just for her?"

"I did."

"After all that, why didn't you marry her?"

"Well, I figured I had become such a clean-cut desirable fellow that I could do better."

Tom: "Would you advise me to marry a beautiful girl or a sensible girl?"

Dick: "I'm afraid you'll never be able to marry either."

Tom: "Why not?"

Dick: "Well, a beautiful girl could do better, and a sensible girl would know better."

A boy came from school and announced: "I'm really in a tough spot. The teacher says I must learn to write more legibly. But if I do, she'll find out I can't spell."

❋   ❋   ❋

"But Professor," challenged the student, "I don't deserve a zero."

"I agree," replied the professor, "but that's the lowest I'm allowed to give."

A little boy asked his father, "Can you be punished for something you didn't do?"

"Of course not," replied his father. "That wouldn't be right."

"Good," said the boy. "Because I didn't do my homework."

A suburbanite sitting at his window early one evening called to his terribly inquisitive wife:

"There goes Peter D'Souza and the woman he's in love with."

His wife dropped the plate she was drying in the kitchen, hurtled through the door, knocked over a lamp and craned her neck to look. "Where?" she panted.

"There," he pointed, "that woman at the corner in the blue coat."

"You idiot," she cried, "that's his wife!"

"Why, of course it is," replied the husband calmly.

✳   ✳   ✳

ST PAULS
by Westminster Cathedral
Morpeth Terrace, London SW1P 1EP
Tel: 020 7828 5582 Fax: 020 7828 3329

VAT No. 207 8496 41   Date 07/07/12

----------------CASH SALE----------------

9788187886341
Images in Mirrors
1 @   3.99   3.99

9781586174897
In Defense of Sanity
1 @   14.99   14.99

TOTAL	:	18.98
EURO TOTAL	:	25.62
CASH	:	20.00
CHANGE	:	1.02

Staff Name KEN   Time 15:22
Receipt No. 1230087   Till No. 10

Reg Charity No. 230945
www.stpauls.org.uk

Mother: "Time to go to Sunday school, Tommy?"

Little boy: "I don't want to go today."

Mother: "Now you be a good boy and get off quick. The teacher will tell you all about heaven."

Little boy: "I don't want him to tell me. I want it to come as a surprise."

✻

At the famous Hyde Park Corner in London, on a Sunday morning, a soap-box speaker was holding forth on the merits of and glories of heaven. "Look here," said a facetious heckler, "what worries me is how I am going to get my shirt on over my wings."

"Don't you worry, my friend," shouted the speaker, "your particular trouble will be getting your trousers on over your tail."

Two friends were meeting each other after a long time. One was using crutches.

"What's the matter with you?" asked the other.

"I had a car accident about six months ago," he explained.

"Don't tell me that you still have to move with crutches."

"As a matter of fact, my doctor says I should stop using them. But then my lawyer says I shouldn't."

✻   ✻   ✻

Jimmy had just got back from the beach.

"Were there other children there?" asked his mother.

"Yes," said Jimmy.

"Boys or girls?"

"How would I know! They didn't have clothes on."

The nun gave a long talk on sin, prayer and forgiveness. When she finished the lesson, she asked little Mary, "What do we have to do before we ask the Lord to forgive us?"

"Sin," replied Mary confidently.

In his autobiography *Treasure in Clay*, Bishop Fulton Sheen records one incident when he lost his way to the Town Hall in Philadelphia. He stopped to ask a few boys who were playing in the street, for directions. After they told him where the Hall was, one of them asked, "What are you going to do there?"

"I'm giving a lecture on heaven and how to get there. Would you like to come and find out?"

"You're kidding," one boy said. "You don't even know the way to the Town Hall!"

✳   ✳   ✳

A father was lecturing his young hopeful on the evils of staying out late at night and getting up late in the morning.

"You will never amount to anything," he concluded, "unless you turn over a new leaf. Remember that the early bird catches the worm."

"How about the worm, father?" inquired the young man. "Wasn't he rather foolish to get up so early?"

"My son," replied the father solemnly, "that worm hadn't been to bed all night; he was on his way home."

One friend said to another one day, "It is good of you to say such pleasant things of Mr Lobo when he always says such nasty things about you."

To which the other replied, "Perhaps we are both mistaken."

A young composer once came to Mozart for advice on how to develop creatively. "Begin writing simple things first," Mozart told him, "songs for example."

"But you composed symphonies when you were only a child," the man exclaimed.

"Ah," Mozart answered, "but I didn't go to anybody to find out how to become a composer."

*   *   *

Samuel Morse is the US inventor of the telegraph. The 'Morse code' — a system of dots and dashes by which telegraphic messages are conveyed — is named after him. There are two interesting anecdotes related to him.

Professor Morse exhibited his telegraphic invention before the United States Congress in 1837, but had to struggle on scanty means till 1843. On the last night of Congress, it voted a substantial sum for the enterprise. The daughter of the Commissioner of Patents brought the news early in the morning to the despondent Morse, and was promised by him the first message over the specially constructed wires between Baltimore and Washington.

The first telegram in the world ran: "WHAT HATH GOD WROUGHT."

Morse was a successful artist as well as an inventor. He once painted a picture of a man in his death agony and showed it to a friend, who happened to be a doctor.

"Well, what's your opinion?" Morse demanded, after the doctor had studied the painting.

"Malaria," said the medical man without hesitation.

*   *   *

D. TWO SIDES

The owner of a chicken farm wanted to make his son behave better, so he devised an object lesson. "Do you see, my son? The chickens that were bad were eaten by a fox."

"So?" replied his son. "If they had been good, *we* would have eaten them."

Two battered old hulks of humanity were sitting on a park bench. One of them leaned over and said to his neighbour, "I'm a man who never took advice from anybody."

"Shake, pal," said the other, "I'm the man who followed everybody's advice."

An interview with a successful business man.
Interviewer: "To what do you attribute your success?"

Business man: "Two words — right decisions."

Interviewer: "How do you make right decisions?"

Business man: "One word — experience."

Interviewer: "How did you get the experience?"

Business man: "Two words — wrong decisions."

✳   ✳   ✳

E. BOOMERANGS

A man had the habit of leaving the cap off the toothpaste tube every morning. His wife who was clearly upset, used to complain to him every now and then, but he continued leaving the tube uncapped. Finally, when they celebrated the Silver Jubilee anniversary of their wedding, the man decided that he would mend his ways. From that day on, he conscientiously began to twist the cap back on.

After a week his wife eyed him suspiciously one morning and asked, "Why have you stopped brushing your teeth?"

Father : "When Rajiv Gandhi was your age, he was head of his class."

Son : "I know. When he was your age, he was Prime Minister."

"There is nothing in the world which is impossible for me," said a mental patient. "I have conquered space and time."

"I'll bet you can't walk up on a beam of light from my flashlight," said the other patient.

"I could do it, but I won't," replied the first patient. "When I got halfway up you'd turn off the light — then where would I be?"

✻   ✻   ✻

A lawyer dropped in at a corner butcher shop and got quite a conversation. "What would you do, sir," asked the butcher, "if a dog kept coming in and stealing meat?"

"Why, I'd make the owner pay for it, of course," replied the lawyer.

"In that case you owe me seventy-five rupees," the butcher said, elated, "because it's your dog."

The lawyer smiled. "Fair enough," he agreed, "just deduct it from the hundred rupees you owe me as consultation fee."

A young business man, who had made it up the social ladder, was deeply in love with a popular and highly respected actress. Over a period of several months, he kept her company, escorting her to restaurants, parties and public functions. Eventually he decided to marry the attractive young lady.

Before making his decision, however, he felt it necessary to investigate her life. He contacted a detective agency, and the job was assigned to a special agent who was not informed about the identity of the client.

Finally, the agency sent him this report: "Miss — has an excellent reputation. Her past is spotless, her associates beyond reproach. The only hint of scandal is that in recent months she has been seen in the company of a business man of doubtful reputation."

* * *

After a long session with the German Chancellor Prince von Bismarck, the British Ambassador asked, "How do you deal with insistent visitors who overextend their welcome?"

Bismarck explained that he had an excellent method. He would make a subtle signal to his aide, who would pass the signal on to a servant. The servant would come in politely and inform him that his wife had an urgent matter to discuss with him.

At that instant, there was a knock at the door and a servant entered with a message from his wife.

After making a public address, the bishop said to the young reporter who was covering the event: "When you do your write-up, I would appreciate it if you didn't mention the several anecdotes I related. I may want to use them in other speeches."

The newsman obliged by inserting this line in his article: "The bishop told several stories which cannot be repeated here."

It was lunch hour at the plant and Pat's two buddies decided to play a little joke on him during his absence. They drew the features of a donkey on the back of his coat. In due time, Pat returned and presently hove in sight bearing the decorated coat.

"What's the trouble, Pat?" asked one casually.

"Nothing much," replied Pat, equally indifferent, "only I'd like to know which of you wiped his face on my coat?"

Teacher: "So you are the boy who wrote on the board, `Teacher is a fool'?"

Pupil: "Yes, sir."

Teacher: "Well, I am glad you have at least told the truth."

The ambitious young woman had managed to wangle an invitation to an important function. She found herself seated between a celebrated bishop and a distinguished rabbi and she was determined to make the most out of this notable company.

"I feel," she said, choosing her words very carefully, "as if I were a leaf between the Old Testament and the New Testament."

"That page, madam," said the rabbi, "is usually blank."

A clergyman, who had accepted an invitation to officiate at Sunday services in a neighbouring town, entrusted his new curate with the performance of his own duties. On returning home, he asked the president of the Women's Sodality what she thought of the curate's sermon. "It was the poorest one I ever heard," she replied. "Nothing in it at all."

Later in the day, the clergyman, meeting his curate, asked how he had got on. "Oh very well," was the reply. "I didn't have time to prepare anything, so I preached one of your unused sermons."

✳　　✳　　✳

Mary : "I hear you have accepted him. Did he happen to mention that he had proposed to me first?"

Jane : "Not specifically. He did say, however, that he had done a lot of foolish things before he met me."

✳

He: "Please, darling, whisper those three little words that will make me walk on air."

She: "Go hang yourself."

✳

Sam told his girl that if she did not marry him he'd get a rope and hang himself right in front of her.

"Oh, please don't do it, Sam," she said. "You know how father doesn't want you hanging around here."

✳

The father's tone was severe as he said: "Young man, do you think you should be taking my daughter to nightclubs all the time?"

"Certainly not," the boy answered, then added hopefully, "let's try to reason with her."

✳

A generous host was overheard telling his friend: "I drank to his health so often that I ruined my own."

✳   ✳   ✳

F. SELF-PROJECTIONS

Dr Norman Vincent Peale had delivered an inspiring speech. As people were congratulating him in the hall, he noticed a woman looking fixedly at him. He went over to her and said, "Madam, did you want to speak to me?"

"Hello, Norman," the woman said, "don't you know me?"

"You have a familiar look," said Dr Peale, "but I can't place you."

"I went to high school with you," she said. "You know, you've done very well with what little you had to start with."

Dr Peale was hurt to the quick by this remark. But after giving some thought to it, he concluded, "You know, that's really what I've been speaking about and writing about all my life: *Do the best you can with what little talent you've got, and you'll go far.*"

An officer was asked by his Company Commander to explain why a report was in error.

"Sir," the junior said, "you've to understand that I have four idiots working for me."

The Company Commander looked up from his desk and said: "You're lucky. I've five idiots working for me."

✳   ✳   ✳

Uncle John came to stay, and before leaving gave his nephew fifty rupees. "Now, be careful with that money, Jimmy," he said. "Remember the saying, `A fool and his money are soon parted'."

"Yes," replied Jimmy, "but I want to thank you for parting with it, just the same."

At a meeting the speaker was getting tired of the constant interruptions.

"We seem to have many fools here," he said. "Wouldn't it be advisable to hear them one at a time?"

"Yes," said a voice. "Get on with your speech."

A man who thought his wife was losing her hearing, one day decided to test it. He walked in quietly through the front door and stood behind her. "Uma," he said, "can you hear me?"

There was no response, so he took a few steps forward, and said again, "Uma, can you hear me?" Still no reply. So he moved even closer to her, and said,

"Uma, can you hear me now?"

"Yes, dear," Uma answered, "for the third time, yes!"

✱   ✱   ✱

When a mother learned that her young son had told a lie she was shocked and decided it was necessary to put the fear of the devil into him in order to convince him to change his ways. When all was quiet that evening, she sat him beside her on the sofa and asked him to pay close attention to her.

"An ugly-looking monster, with sharp horns on his head and fire streaming out of his eyes snatches all children who tell lies and carries them away. He takes them to a distant planet and makes them do hard work day and night, beating them if they disobey his commands. Only when they get very old does he bring them back to their family."

Feeling satisfied that she had made an impression on the lad, she concluded, "You will not tell lies any more, will you?"

"I guess not, Mum," said the boy, "You tell better ones."

"Don't ever visit the night-club," said a father, as a warning to his teenaged son."

"Why not?" challenged the boy.

"Because you'll see things that you shouldn't."

The lad's curiosity was aroused, so once he stole into the nightclub. And there he saw something he shouldn't have — his own father.

Honest people alter their
ideas to fit the truth,
and dishonest people alter
the truth to fit their ideas.

There were two boys who were good friends; one, however, was totally blind. Strolling in a park one evening, they came across a woman selling baskets of *jambuls* (a fruit the size of cherries). The seeing one suggested to his blind friend that they chip in and buy a basket. As they sat on a bench to enjoy the fruit, they made an agreement. In order that each has an equal share of the basket, they would take turns in eating one jambul at a time.

They sampled the jambuls for a few minutes. Suddenly, the blind boy struck out wildly, hitting his friend on the nose. "What's that for?" cried the surprised friend. "Did I do anything wrong?"

"You are cheating me," rasped the blind one. "I've been taking two jambuls at a time and you haven't said a word. So you must be taking three or four at a time or you would have complained. I didn't suspect you would be such a cheat!"

While out on a stroll, a young boy asked his father how electricity went through the lighting wires. "I don't know, son," said the father. "I have not learned much about electricity."

Since the sky was overcast and there was a spark in the sky, the boy asked his dad how lightning and thunder were caused. "As a matter of fact," said the man truthfully, "I have never understood that myself."

"Say, dad," began the boy after a while. "Oh, well, never mind."

"Go ahead," said the father. "Ask questions. Ask a lot of questions. How else are you going to learn?"

❋   ❋   ❋

G. FOOT IN THE MOUTH

Clerk (to customer): "No, ma'am, we haven't had any for a long time."

Owner (angrily breaking in): "We have plenty in reserve, ma'am, plenty downstairs."

The customer bursts into laughter and leaves the shop.

Owner: "What did she say to you?"

Clerk: "We haven't had any rain lately."

Shop owner: "What's the problem? Remember, in this store, the customer is always right. What did the young lady say?"

"She said the owner of this shop is a damn fool."

"Your methods of cultivation are hopelessly out of date," said the agricultural student to the old farmer. "I would be surprised if you got even ten pounds of apples from that tree."

"I would be surprised, too," said the farmer, "considering that is a pear tree."

✳   ✳   ✳

"Did anyone call when I was out?" asked the boss.

"Yes, sir," answered the secretary. "There was a guy who called a few minutes ago, threatening to beat you up."

"What did you tell him?"

"I told him I was very sorry that you weren't in."

At a party one man turned to the other and said, "Who is that awful looking lady in the corner?"

"What! That's my wife," said the second man.

"Oh, I didn't mean her," recovered the first man, "I mean the lady next to her."

"That," cried the second man, "is my daughter."

At the same party, a young lady had just been introduced to her partner for a dance. By way of making conversation she said, "Who is that terribly ugly looking man over there?"

"Why, that's my brother!" he exclaimed.

"Oh! you must excuse me," said the lady in embarrassment and added apologetically, "I really hadn't noticed the resemblance."

❊   ❊   ❊

There is the story told of a priest who was hearing the confessions of children. He was very puzzled when practically every child, after reciting the more familiar and intelligible sins, accused themselves of "throwing peanuts in the river." The priest wondered whether they were repenting of wasting food or of river pollution. When the last and smallest child came in, he decided to press for a little more explanation. But the smallest penitent failed to confess this. "Yes," said the priest, "is that all — isn't there something you've forgotten? What about throwing peanuts in the river?"

"But, Father," said a bewildered voice, "I am Peanuts."

"How is your wife?" the man asked a friend he hadn't seen for years.

"She's in heaven," replied the friend.

"Oh, I'm sorry." Then he realised that was not the thing to say, so he added, "I mean, I'm glad." And that was even worse. He finally came out with, "Well, I'm surprised."

A young man lying on a hospital stretcher just before his operation turned to a sympathetic lady who stood near by and said, "I'm so nervous. This is my first operation."

"So am I," said the lady. "My husband is the doctor and it is his first operation too."

✳　　✳　　✳

H. POINTING A FINGER

New tenants had moved into the house across the street from a woman who was something of a snob.

When her husband came home from work, she remarked: "Those new people don't have a piano or a television set or even a car."

"Well," the husband muttered, "maybe they have a bank account."

A woman customer had been trying the patience of the clerk, and he began to lose his temper.

"Please get the manager," the woman ordered. "Perhaps he has a little more sense than you."

"He does, madam. He left when you came in."

The local lush asked Father Fernandes one day what sciatica was. The priest, thinking this was a good opportunity to teach him a lesson, said: "My good man, sciatica is usually caused by too much carousing and drinking and chasing girls! Why do you ask? Do you have it bad?"

"Oh, no, Father," answered the reprobate. "I haven't got it at all. I was just reading in the paper that a certain Bishop has it."

✳   ✳   ✳

A clergyman and one of his elderly parishioners were walking home from church one frosty day when the old gentleman slipped and fell flat on his back. The minister looked at him for a moment and, being assured that he was not hurt, said to him, "Friend, sinners stand on slippery places."

The old gentleman looked up as if to assure himself of the fact and said, "I see they do, but I can't."

One of the points made by a principal of a school when instructing new recruits to the staff was:

"The red-pencil mentality is highly contagious. We all seem to catch the habit of looking for the flaw, the mistake, the awkward and the ugly in others."

Master: "Why didn't you deliver that message as instructed?"

Servant: "I did the best I could, sir."

Master: "The best you could! If I'd known I was sending a stupid idiot, I would have gone myself!"

The best place to criticise
is in front of your own mirror.

I. UNKIND CUTS

In an apartment building, seeing a woman struggling up the stairs with a load of packages, a young man offered to help her. When they reached her door on the sixth floor, she thanked the man, then asked suddenly, "Do you smoke?"

"Yes, thanks, I do."

"I thought so. You are awfully out of breath for your age."

Riding a crowded bus home from work, a young man found a seat and was reluctant to give it up, although a woman standing near him was glaring accusingly. Finally, his conscience brought him to his feet.

"Would you like to have my seat, Madam?" he asked chivalrously.

"It's *Miss*," she snapped and took the seat.

Woman: "Are you the young man who risked his life to save my son from drowning when he fell over the bridge?"

Man : "Yes, ma'am."

Woman: "Well, what did you do with his socks?"

✳   ✳   ✳

A certain low-income worker, Mr Jones, who had won millions of pounds in a lottery, decided that he and his wife should take a very grand holiday. After much deliberation, they settled for a round-the-world cruise on a liner of extreme luxury. They loaded themselves with luggage and reserved the largest and most expensive suite on the ship.

When the Captain scanned his passenger-list to find the most influential people to dine at his table, he came across Mr Jones' name. And, on enquiring, he was told that he had booked the No 1 suite. Here seemed the right man and the Captain sent the Chief Steward to the Jones' cabin with an invitation to join him for dinner.

The steward was extremely surprised to receive the following reply: "What? I spend a fortune to get the finest and best suite on this beautiful ship and now I'm expected to eat with the crew?"

A drunk shuffled up to a rich banker and asked for a rupee for a cup of coffee. Being an extremely generous man, the banker handed him a twenty-rupee note. "Here," he said, "you can buy yourself twenty cups of coffee with that."

Next evening the banker saw the drunken tramp again. "How are you today?" he asked cheerfully.

The tramp glared at him. "Why don't you get lost," he said rudely. "You and your twenty cups of coffee. They left me awake all last night."

If you have nothing for which
to be thankful, be sure there's
something wrong with you.

J. KINDNESS REBOUNDS

Little Tommy came home from school with a black eye.

"What have you been up to?" demanded his mother.

"I've been fighting Danny," the boy confessed.

"Well, tomorrow morning take him some cake and make friends," his mother told him.

Tommy did so, but the following afternoon he came home with the other eye blacked. "Good heavens!" exploded his mother, "who did that?"

"Danny did," said Tommy. "He wants more cake."

A fat old lady said to a fellow-traveller on a train: "Sir, will you help me off the train at the next station?"

"Certainly, madam."

"You see, I'm so stout, I've to get off the train backwards; but every time I try to do so, people think I'm getting on and give me a shove. I'm four stations passed my destination already."

Kindness is the ability to
love people more than they
really deserve.

A young burglar fleeing across a rooftop heard the crash of glass behind him. Looking back, he saw a policeman falling through a skylight. The 26-year-old thief went back and supported the officer until help came. Then he was arrested and sentenced to twenty months in prison.

Four months later, a judge reviewed the case, saluted the man's "outstanding gallantry" and set him free. Headlines heralded the former burglar as a hero.

He soon found that public esteem was short-lived. Every attempt to get a permanent job met with failure. Three employers discharged him when they learned of his past. Nine others refused to hire him because he told the full truth at job interviews.

The embittered man complained: "If I hadn't stayed to save that policeman's life, I would probably not be in this fix now. But I'll never go back to crime."

A group of staff members were walking along a pathway outside a college, when they noticed a large cardboard box right in the middle of it. One of them being a public-spirited person, strode forward to move it out of the way. No sooner had he picked it up and taken another step forward than he disappeared.

He had fallen into a deep hole which another public-spirited person had covered with the box.

*   *   *

Collecting fares, the bus-conductor stopped beside a small boy, who felt in all his pockets and looked under his seat while the conductor was waiting.

"What's the trouble, sonny?" he asked.

"I had a rupee and I've lost it."

The little fellow looked so upset that the conductor gave him the ticket free.

The boy looked up, and on the point of tears, whimpered, "And what about my change?"

Four good fellows, old friends, met after long years in an Irish provincial town. They visited an inn and had several drinks. Then all four left for the railway station.

The train was about to leave and the three stood unsteadily at the door of a carriage. The station-master, who happened to be near, managed to shove three of them in just as the train was pulling out. The fourth fellow standing on the platform began to laugh until he was weak.

The station master asked, "What the heck are you laughing at?"

The stranded passenger replied, "Well, they were supposed to be seeing me off!"

❋　　❋　　❋

One 82-year-old man who took on the job of Santa Claus at a store during Christmas put so much enthusiasm into his role that he found himself out of work.

The pensioner was paid to sit in his red coat and white beard in the store in a poor neighbourhood and speak kindly to the shy children

When they would whisper their wishes in his ear, however, he began to melt. "I couldn't bear to see them go away disappointed," he said later. "There were a lot of toys on the shelves nearby that no one seemed to be buying. So I started handing them to some of the children as an extra present."

While store officials sympathised with the sentiment, they insisted on the hard facts of commercial life. The old man was politely sacked.

Every morning a train commuter dropped 50 paisa on the tray of a man selling pencils at the station, but he never took any pencils. One day, when he put down his usual 50 paisa, the beggar touched him on the shoulder.

"It's all right," said the traveller. "I don't want any pencils."

"It's not that, sir," said the beggar. "The price of pencils has gone up to one rupee."

* * *

K. SERIOUS QUESTIONS

A curious young girl once asked her mother at a wedding, "Why is the bride dressed in white?"

"Because the colour white is a sign of happiness," her mother explained. "For the bride, today is the happiest day of her life."

The child let the thought sink in. She stared at the newly-weds, and asked her mother again. "If that's the case for the bride, why is the groom wearing black?"

In a comic strip *B.C.* by Johnny Hart, the character Wiley asks a searching question: "Whatever happened to kindness?" and then proceeds to write the following verse:

Why do people go to the trouble
　　to give other people some trouble?
Why do they burst someone's bubble
　　when they know it comes back to them double?
Why do we go to the effort to hurt
　　someone we actually love?
Why can't we say something sweet 'stead of curt?
　　A push leads to a shove.
Why can't we treat other folks with respect?
　　With a smile or a kind word or two? ...
Why can't we overlook others' mistakes?
　　We've all surely been there before.

✳　✳　✳

In times past, in a certain city in China, there lived a man who sold military weapons. "My shields are so solid," he boasted, "that nothing can pierce them. My spears are so sharp that there is nothing they can't penetrate."

So someone challenged him: "What happens when one of your spears strikes one of your shields?"

The man was dumbfounded.

Mistress: "And, above all, I want obedience and truthfulness."

New maid: "Yes, madam. But, if anybody calls when you are in and you want me to say you are out, which comes first: obedience or truthfulness?"

The father decided to have a serious talk with young Tommy, who was inclined to be light-hearted and irresponsible.

"Tommy," he said, "you're getting to be a big boy and you ought to take things more seriously. Just think if I died suddenly, where would you be?"

"Here," answered Tommy. "The question is, where would you be?"

✵   ✵   ✵

"Look here, waiter, is this peach-pie or apple-pie?"

"Can't you tell from the taste?"

"No, I can't."

"Well, then, what difference does it make?"

A mother was telling her six-year-old about the Golden Rule:

"Always remember," she said, "that we're here to help others."

"Well, what are the others here for?" asked the little girl.

"You are one for asking questions, aren't you?" said the father. "I'd like to know what would have happened if I'd asked as many questions when I was a boy."

"Perhaps," suggested the young fellow, "you'd have been able to answer some of mine."

There are two sides to every
question, except when it
happens to be a love-triangle.

PERSONS AND POSSESSIONS

It's pretty hard to tell
what brings happiness;
poverty and wealth
have both failed.

A. HITTING THE JACKPOT

A 39-year-old Sydney factory worker and mother of five won 15.34 million dollars (U.S. $ 11 million) in a lottery, the biggest-ever Australian lotto jackpot, November 1997. Jane was working the afternoon shift at the assembly-line in the factory and was unaware of her win until she saw signs about the unclaimed prize outside her local news agency. After rushing home to check her ticket, she realised she was the winner.

Her struggling family, living in the blacktown western suburbs, celebrated with dinner at a restaurant. They plan to pay off their 40,000 — dollar debts, buy two cars, spend a family holiday at Disneyland and in Greece, and buy a diamond ring!

A story of ancient times tells of a king who had a huge boulder placed in the middle of a busy road in his kingdom and hid himself to see the reactions. Rich merchants cursed loudly as their chariots veered off the road to avoid the boulder. A poor farmer, however, put down the sack of grain he was carrying on his back, and after much pushing and straining managed to get the boulder off the road.

To his surprise, half buried in a hole, where the boulder had been, was a bag containing gold coins. A soldier appeared and told him it was his reward for removing the boulder.

B. ATTITUDES

One day a little girl asked her mother who was a popular interviewer on TV, how she had such a pleasant appearance on the small screen, but always had a sour demeanour when at home.

"Well, you know," answered the mother, "the TV people pay me for smiling."

"I see," said the innocent child reflectively. "Mummy, how much would you have to be paid to smile at home?"

The mother's eyes suddenly swelled with tears. She embraced her little one and said: "From now on, I'll do it for nothing."

Husband: "I'm going to take on as many jobs as I can, and one day we are going to be very rich."

Wife: "We are rich already, dear, because we have each other.... Some day we may have money."

A young man stood quietly at the bedside of his dying father. "Please, my boy," whispered the old man, "always remember that wealth does not bring happiness."

"Yes, father," said the man, "I realise that, but at least it will allow me to choose the kind of misery I find most agreeable."

❈   ❈   ❈

The story is told of a man who entered the office of the priest's residence at a local church and demanded in a haughty tone: "I want to see the head hog."

"Excuse me, sir," the secretary chided, "we don't refer to our priest with any nicknames."

"I don't care what you call the old boy," the man insisted. "I want to see the head hog."

"Let me put it another way," said the secretary. "Our pastor has a good standing in this parish. No one would want to call him any nickname, much less that of a pig."

"Listen, lady," said the proud gentleman pulling a cheque out of his pocket. "I would like to donate three lakhs of rupees to the church. Now can I see the head hog?"

"Goodness me," exclaimed the secretary, "I think I hear the little porker coming now."

A wealthy man was on his deathbed. He called the priest and asked him: "If I donate a hundred million rupees to the church, will I get to heaven?"

The priest answered: "There is no harm in trying, though I cannot guarantee you anything. Your wealth is going to be left behind, so why not try?"

There's nothing wrong with you possessing riches. The wrong comes with riches possessing you.

When Colleen McCullough worked on *The Thorn Birds* she was a struggling medical researcher in Australia, badly in need of funds. On submitting her manuscript to a publisher, McCullough decided to get the background for a hospital novel, so she went to England to enter nurse's training. "I didn't tell them I wrote books, of course," she said. "I was looking forward to some really hard physical labour because I am a workaholic."

The training was scheduled to begin on April 11, 1977. However, on February 27 of that year, *The Thorn Birds* made a record sale. "I hit the headlines everywhere," McCullough recalled. "I could no longer go on nursing. Can you imagine a millionairess author carrying a bedpan!"

Jack Benny, the American comedian, who was highly successful in vaudeville, radio, television and films, often made jokes about stinginess. In one episode, Jack is confronted by a thief. The thief puts a gun to Benny's head and says, "Your life or your money?"

Benny does not respond. So the thief repeats, "Your life or your money?" This is followed by silence. The thief begins to lose his patience, and says in a strong voice, "I said, `Your life or your money?' Which will it be?"

Benny replies, "Give me time, I'm still thinking."

Wealth is a worry if you
have it, and a worry if
you don't have it.

C. DETACHMENT

An elderly person remarked: "Up to the age of 20, I owned little more than my clothes, my pride and my appetite. From 20 to 50, I was like a magpie and brought home everything I fancied and could afford. From 50 to 60 I sat and looked and enjoyed what was mine; but between 60 and 70, I found my enjoyment lay in giving my possessions away. Now, at 70, my three-score and ten, I find only three possessions worth keeping: my Bible, my spectacles and my false teeth."

Barbara McClintock did pioneering work for forty long years in the field of science before she was awarded the Nobel Prize. During those years she went through a rough spell. Sceptical scientists questioned her findings and for decades denied her validity. "They called me crazy, absolutely mad at times," she recalls. But she carried on doggedly, never doubting she had a contribution to make to humanity.

Finally, at the age of 79, when heaped with honours and material rewards, McClintock commented: "These things never have been important to me. I never wanted to be bothered by possessions. When I was much younger, I used to say I wanted two things — to own an automobile and spectacles. Now I just want my spectacles."

Contentment in life consists
not in great wealth but in
simple wants.

There is a highly inspiring story by Nil Guillemette, S.J., entitled *King Pluto : How To Become Rich In One Easy Lesson.* Here is a condensed version.

King Pluto's coffers were overflowing with the proceeds of the taxes he levied, and with the presents of those who sought his favours and with the tribute offerings of those who feared his power. He believed he was the richest man in the world, and the thought made him glad.

One day, however, while parading the streets of the capital in his gilded carriage, he noticed some beggars receiving money from the passers-by. This image haunted him and set him thinking. Whatever wealth he had, had been given to him out of obligation, self-interest, or fear. What the beggars received was given out of sheer compassion, and had greater value.

King Pluto decided to disguise himself and beg at the doors of shrines and churches every Sunday. He did this for many years and put away the money he received in alms in a special box. When he had collected enough, he abdicated his throne, and travelled to a distant land as a stranger, and bought a modest farm. Now he believed that he was truly the richest man in the world, because all he owed was given to him freely, out of sheer compassion.

Eventually, Pluto's gentle manners and fund of stories and anecdotes made him popular with the local children, and very friendly with the neighbours. Pluto's favourite was Ani, the seven-year-old son of his nearest neighbour. Ani's family was poor, and Ani had no toys. All he owned was a nightingale he had captured and tamed. His greatest joy was to listen to the nightingale sing before he went to bed.

One day Pluto was seized by a strange illness. To cheer him, Ani gifted Pluto his only possession — the nightingale. That night, while listening to the bird sing, Pluto suddenly realised what this gift meant to him. It was true that he had bought the farm with the alms he had received. But then, the alms were given to him — a faceless beggar — out of compassion.

The nightingale, however, was given to him for what he was as a person, out of love. Surely this act made it something special, and he could now count himself truly as the richest person in the world.

When he recovered from his illness, Pluto learned that a poor farmer in the town, who had seven children, could not pay back what he had borrowed from money-lenders. The judge had ordered his farm to be taken over. Pluto loved the family and did not want to see it reduced to misery. So Pluto sold his own property and arranged for the proceeds to be given to the poor farmer to cover his debts.

Then quietly, he took to the road once again, penniless. But his heart was filled with a feeling of fulfilment. He said to himself: "This time I know I am the richest man in the world."

A foreign tourist made a special trip to the residence of the learned Polish rabbi, Hofetz Chaim. On entering the rabbi's house he was astonished to see it practically bare, except for a table, a work-bench, and some shelves of books.

"Rabbi, where is all your furniture?" asked the tourist.

"Where is yours?" replied the rabbi.

"Mine? Why, I'm a visitor here. I'm only passing through."

"So am I," said the rabbi.

The greatest wealth is
contentment with a little.

Young priest: "Monsignor, your trousers are in an awful state. Why not get a new pair?"

Monsignor (aged 90) : "Can't afford them."

Priest : "Of course you can; you've got plenty of money in the bank, and you can't take it with you when you die."

Monsignor : "Can't take my trousers, either."

A priest was at the bedside of a miser who was dying.

"Ah," cried the miser feebly. "If I could only take my gold with me."

"No use," said the priest. "It would melt."

One : "Money buys happiness."

Other : "I don't agree."

One : "Wouldn't a little more money make you a little happier?"

Other : "I believe so."

> *If happiness could be bought,*
> *most of us would be unhappy*
> *because of the price.*

D. PERCEPTIONS

A wealthy merchant was exceedingly miserly and refused to help a poor family who were in need of food and medicine. The local priest decided to confront him. One day, while visiting the merchant, the priest took out a mirror and asked the man to look into it. "What do you see?" asked the priest.

"My face, of course," answered the man.

Then the priest asked him to look through the glass panel of the window. "What do you see?" asked the priest again.

"Trees, shacks, children playing in the street.... Why do you ask?"

"Through the window you see life, in the mirror you see yourself," explained the man of God. Both the window and the mirror have glass, but the mirror is coated with silver. Silver conceals your view of life; it reflects only yourself. That is what wealth does to a person."

As understanding dawned, the miser hung his head in shame and said, "You are right, I have been blinded by silver. I will make amends."

A person once confided to a friend: "When I was fourteen I decided that I was going to become the richest man in the world, whatever the cost."

"What happened then?" asked the friend.

"By the time I was twenty-one I thought it is easier to change my mind than to become the richest man in the world."

There was a business man who was deeply religious and extremely charitable. He was known as the 'cheerful giver' because of his deep sense of humour. Naturally, he was loved by everyone. One day calamity struck. He was badly cheated by his investors, and he was almost completely ruined financially. As soon as news of this got around, a delegation of his beneficiaries, believing that the man would be sad and depressed and need some cheering up, called on him. To their amazement, they found the merchant serenely engrossed in his studies.

"Sir," they exclaimed, "how is it possible that you can be so calm? You have lost all your wealth. Don't you ever worry?'

"Of course, I do," answered the afflicted man. "But i thank God for blessing me with a quick mind. You see, the worrying that others do in a month takes me only about a half hour."

Henry Ford once asked a young engineer what his main ambition in life was. The man confessed that he wanted to become very wealthy. Some days later, when Ford came across the young man again, he pulled out a pair of metal-rimmed spectacles which had a pair of silver dollars in place of glass lenses. He told the engineer to put them on. Then he asked him what he could see with them.

"Nothing," replied the young man. "The money blocks out the view."

"Don't you think you should reconsider that ambition of yours?" said Ford, and walked away.

Watch out for the ambition
to get rich. It can get you
into a lot of hard work.

In the days gone by, there was a tiny village lost in the hills, whose inhabitants had hardly any contact with the outside modernised world. One day, a man from the neighbouring city arrived in the village square in order to recruit labourers. A few opportunistic youth decided to go. As one of them, a newly married man, bade farewell to his young wife, he asked her what she would like him to bring back from the city. "Oh, anything you please," she said shyly. "Only, make sure it is something pretty, as pretty as the moon."

After the job was over, and it was time for the labourers to return, the young man went to the city market. The large stores and the attractive window-displays dazzled him. He had a hard time deciding what gift he could take his wife. Suddenly his eyes fell upon something which exactly reflected his wife's desires. It was a round mirror, shaped like the moon.

As soon as he arrived home he presented the gift to his attractive wife. She was overawed by the delicate tissue paper and ribbons, and unwrapped the present with delicate hands. Then she held up the mirror to her face and suddenly found herself looking at the image of a lovely maiden. She stared at it speechlessly for a while, then ran out the door at great speed.

Her confounded husband followed in hot pursuit. The girl kept running till she arrived at her paternal house, and then called out, "Mother, mother, my husband does not love me anymore. Look. He has brought me a beautiful girl from the city."

"Where is she," asked the astounded mother looking around.

"Right here," said the sobbing wife. "You can look for yourself."

The aged woman, who, like the girl, had not seen a mirror before, peered into the looking glass. She, too, was wonderstruck and surprised. After studying the image carefully she handed the mirror back to her daughter and said reassuringly: "My child, you have absolutely nothing to be bothered about. No young man who is in his senses would ever sacrifice a beautiful damsel like you for an ugly old woman."

❀   ❀   ❀

E. CLINGING

A fund-raiser visited the wealthiest man of the metropolis and asked for a donation for a Lepers Home. The man refused point-blank.

"You must understand," explained the rich man, "I have a 91-year-old mother who has been in a nursing home for the last eight years. I have a daughter who has been widowed for three years and is struggling to support her five children. Two of my brothers have taken loans from the government and are unable to pay them back...."

"I'm sorry," interrupted the fund-raiser. "I didn't realise you had such great financial responsibilities."

"Oh, no, I didn't mean that," replied the rich man. "I was only trying to tell you that when I don't give any of them one single paisa, why should I give you anything?"

A miserly millionaire knew he was about to die, so he instructed his wife to place a large box containing money, in the room on the top floor. He warned everyone in the family not to touch it. His plan, he said, was "to grab it on my way to heaven." Everyone took care not to shift the box.

When he died, his wife rushed to the room and found the box still there. "He's a real fool," she muttered to herself, "if only he had listened to me and put the box in the basement!"

> *Money may be used as a*
> *universal passport to every-*
> *where except heaven.*

F. CRAVING

In an October 1997 issue of *India Today* there is a story on Dimpy, a criminal from Punjab. Dimpy, the son of a Jat Sikh farmer, went to the State capital Chandigarh for studies in 1990. He eventually got involved in gun-running for Punjab militants, earned his first lakh of rupees, and blew it all on fast cars and a lavish life-style. Once he had tasted the good life, he craved for more money, and wanted it as quickly as possible.

In 1996, Dimpy executed his first kidnapping, and earned his share of Rs 50 lakh from it. He bought a wine business and an industry with part of the wealth. He even floated his own gang, comprising unemployed youth. But soon he became greedy." I wanted to live a royal life," he told a reporter. "I wanted to make quick money through one or two big ransoms."

When he tried to extort money from a businessman he had kidnapped in Bangalore, his telephone call was traced, and he was arrested. He is now languishing in prison.

Some have too much, yet still do crave;
I little have, and seek no more:
They are but poor, though much they have,
And I am rich with little store:
They poor, I rich; they beg, I give;
They lack, I leave; they pine, I live.

E. Dyer

*Not he who has little, but he
who wishes for more, is poor.*

Fritz Kreisler, the great American concert violinist said:

I was born with music in my system. It was a gift from God. I didn't acquire it. So I do not even deserve thanks for the music. Music is too sacred to be sold, and the outrageous prices charged by musical celebrities today are truly a crime against society.

I never look upon the money I earn as my own. It is public money. It is only a fund entrusted to me for proper disbursement. My beloved wife feels exactly as I do.... In all these years of so-called success in music we have not built a house for ourselves. Between it and us stand all the homeless of the world.

Two friends met on a street.

"I've been feeling very unhappy these days," said one.

"Why?" asked the other.

"Two weeks ago my uncle died and left me a million rupees."

"And why should that make you sad?"

"I should be happy, I know," said the friend. "But last week another uncle died and left me two million rupees."

"You should be thrilled."

"I know," said the first, "but every time I keep saying to myself, `I have no more uncles.'"

> *It's difficult to be content if*
> *you don't have enough, and it's*
> *impossible if you have too much.*

G. DIRE CONSEQUENCES

An October 1997 issue of *India Today* contains an interview with 42-year-old Jayaram Basan, owner of *Sagar*, a 10-restaurant chain in Delhi, which is famous for South Indian dishes. Basan, a migrant from Mangalore, earns about Rs 70 lakh a month. But with wealth and fame came an "invisible visitor" — envy. Basan has been constantly abused and threatened by criminal gangs from Uttar Pradesh. Basan lives in constant fear of being kidnapped, even killed.

"I lead a life of relentless agony," he says, as four armed guards keep watch. "I can't take a walk in the park. My kids can't play like other kids. I fear for my family all the time."

Edith Sitwell, in her book *The Eccentrics*, tells of a miser who descended to the vault of his house to gloat over his treasures and found himself walled in by the falling of a trap door. Search was made everywhere for him without success. At last it was given up and the house sold.

The new owner wished to make some alterations in the cellar and the workmen found the miser surrounded by glittering gold and jewels. Beside him lay a candlestick empty because the candle had been eaten. In the pangs of famine the miser had gnawed the flesh from both his arms.

Wealth may not bring happiness
but it seems to bring a pleasant
kind of misery.

G. DIRE CONSEQUENCES

An October 1997 issue of *India Today* contains an interview with 42-year-old Jayaram Basan, owner of *Sagar*, a 10-restaurant chain in Delhi, which is famous for South Indian dishes. Basan, a migrant from Mangalore, earns about Rs 70 lakh a month. But with wealth and fame came an "invisible visitor" — envy. Basan has been constantly abused and threatened by criminal gangs from Uttar Pradesh. Basan lives in constant fear of being kidnapped, even killed.

"I lead a life of relentless agony," he says, as four armed guards keep watch. "I can't take a walk in the park. My kids can't play like other kids. I fear for my family all the time."

Edith Sitwell, in her book *The Eccentrics*, tells of a miser who descended to the vault of his house to gloat over his treasures and found himself walled in by the falling of a trap door. Search was made everywhere for him without success. At last it was given up and the house sold.

The new owner wished to make some alterations in the cellar and the workmen found the miser surrounded by glittering gold and jewels. Beside him lay a candlestick empty because the candle had been eaten. In the pangs of famine the miser had gnawed the flesh from both his arms.

> *Wealth may not bring happiness*
> *but it seems to bring a pleasant*
> *kind of misery.*

C. DIRE CONSEQUENCES

An October 1997 issue of India Today contains an interview with 42-year-old Jivaram Basan, owner of Sagar, a 10-restaurant chain in Delhi, which is famous for South Indian dishes. Basan, a migrant from Mangalore, earns about Rs 70 lakh a month. But with wealth and fame came an "invisible visitor" — envy. Basan has been constantly abused and threatened by criminal gangs from Uttar Pradesh. Basan lives in constant fear of being kidnapped, even killed.

"I lead a life of relentless agony," he says, as four armed guards keep watch. "I can't take a walk in the park. My kids can't play like other kids. I fear for my family all the time."

Edith Sitwell, in her book, The Eccentrics, tells of a miser who descended to the vault of his house to gloat over his treasures and found himself walled in by the falling of a trap door. Search was made everywhere for him without success. At last it was given up and the house sold.

The new owner wished to make some alterations in the cellar and the workmen found the miser surrounded by glittering gold and jewels. Beside him lay a candle-stick empty because the candle had been eaten. In the pages of a book the miser had gnawed the flesh from both his arms.

Wealth may not bring happiness
But it generally brings a person
mind of misery